23 and Debt Free

*Our top 50 tips to cutting costs and stretching dollars –
the key to my husband and me becoming debt free in
our mid-twenties.*

By: Annika Joy Caldwell
with W. Logan Caldwell

23 and Debt Free

*"The free bird leaps
on the back of the wind
and floats downstream
till the current ends
and dips his wings
in the orange sun rays
and dares to claim the sky."*

~ Maya Angelou's 'The Caged Bird'

May you discover within the pages of this book the invigorating, hope-filled freedom of the free bird. May you soar from any cages that hold you back and dare to boldly claim your financial freedom. And may the freedom you find grant you the opportunity to live, to dream, and to give.

Copyright © 2018 by Annika Joy Caldwell

All rights reserved. No part of this publication may be reproduced or transmitted in any form or by any means electronic or mechanical, including photocopy, recording, or any information storage and retrieval system without permission in writing from the author, except by a reviewer who wishes to use brief passages in connection with a review written for inclusion in a website, or other media formats.

ISBN 978-1-790-96590-8

Manufactured in the United States of America.

Cover photos: *Elevate Studios*
Book cover design: *Made Midwest*
Author photo: *Beth Ann Photography*

"For if you remain silent at this time, relief and deliverance for the Jews will arise from another place, but you and your father's family will perish. And who knows but that you have come to your royal position for such a time as this?" ~ Esther 4:14 (NIV)

"Give no sleep to your eyes, nor slumber to your eyelids; Deliver yourself like a gazelle from the hunter's hand and like a bird from the hand of the fowler." ~ Proverbs 6:4-5 (NAS)

This book is dedicated to…

My mom, who instilled in me from a young age the tools to set and accomplish my goals. You have always encouraged me to dream big, and I know without having the encouragement to do just that, this book would not have become a reality. I love you, Mom.

And to our two beautiful little girls and the little one who will be joining our family later this year. Although you are far too young to know this, you too inspired this journey. You inspired your Daddy and me to work harder than we've ever worked before to ensure that we can provide the best for you. As your Momma, I pray that you all grow up aware of the many blessings God has given our family – blessings that He has bestowed upon us trusting that we will be good stewards of those blessings. I pray that we as parents have the opportunity to show you the world and to make memories together, but that we also impart on you an attitude of gratitude and show you the beauty of giving – gifts given from God's blessings. May you continue to grow in your faith, and may we never hesitate to tell you our story and to guide you on the path that God has designed just for you. I love you, my children.

table of contents

Introduction 1
Our Story 5
Chapter 1: A Written Plan is Necessary 11
Chapter 2: Children Are Expensive! 19
Chapter 3: Food: The Budget Buster 51
Chapter 4: All Things Insurance 91
Chapter 5: The Costs of Home Ownership 107
Chapter 6: Let Go of the Splurges 123
Chapter 7: Don't Feel Guilty: Holidays and Celebrations on a Budget ... 141
Chapter 8: Rapid Fire: Bonus Tips for Slashing Costs 153
Chapter 9: Giving on a Budget 175
Closing: Not the End, But Rather a Beginning 185
Annika's Testimony 191
Notes 195

introduction

I am about to share with you a book that came to be following our family's journey to become debt free. Our journey seemed long at times, but God granted us strength, encouragement from family and friends, and perseverance to see this journey to completion. Since becoming debt free, He has given us a number of opportunities to reach, encourage, and inspire others with our story.

We are praying that this book does the same. We hope and pray that this book encourages other individuals and couples who are on debt-free journeys similar to our own. And, if you are reading this and are not paying off any debt, but need encouragement and the hope of being able to cut costs for a more secure financial situation, we hope this book speaks to you as well!

We have written this book, not only with the intention of sharing our top 50 tips for cutting costs for yourself and/or your family, but also with the intention of sharing some of our stories. These are stories that we pray will inspire you and give you hope that you, too, can achieve your financial goals and dreams.

Before going any farther, I do have a few people I want to thank for making this book possible.

First and foremost, thank you to my husband, Logan. You are the one who inspired both our debt-free journey and the creation of this book. You encouraged me as I wrote, offered your expertise to write sections of this book, spent hours editing, and continually nagged me to finish this book when my progress slowed.

Thank you to so many of my friends who spent time reading and re-reading this book. When I had stared at the words on these pages for hours, and I was missing the simplest of grammatical errors, you all swept in to help me see these words and this message in a fresh light. My dream of launching this book during my 25th year would never have been accomplished without your dedication.

Thank you to my amazing graphic designer, Angela, at Made Midwest not only for all of your work on this book, but also for all of the time you dedicated to helping us give an image to our story. When Angela began designing our logo, she suggested that we incorporate a bird cage to symbolize the freedom that comes with being debt free. That open bird cage is pictured throughout this book as a reminder to you, the reader, of the freedom that will come from your journey. Angela, I am so grateful to you for the wisdom, insight, and vision that you brought to this project. You are truly an artist!

Thank you to Corey at Elevate Studios for your awesome work capturing the photo for this book cover. My time spent in the studio with you was wonderful. You were encouraging, so attentive to detail, and really made my vision a reality.

Thank you to all of our family and friends who provided encouragement, prayers, hand-me-down girls clothing, free babysitting, and so many other gifts throughout our debt-free journey. You helped us achieve our goal and kept us focused when we were feeling defeated.

Thank you to our awesome Financial Peace University discussion groups and our co-coordinators, Jack and Wanda. We were absolutely honored to do FPU with all of you. You blessed us with your stories and your enthusiasm. Thanks for always holding us accountable and for being some of our best cheerleaders.

Thank you to my amazing bible study ladies. Many of you knew nothing of this book prior to it launching, but that didn't matter. You too were a part of this story. You have encouraged me throughout our entire journey – not just our debt-free journey, but my journey as a wife and a mom as well. I cannot say enough to thank you all for being an amazing group of supportive, loving, vulnerable, honest, broken, goal-oriented women. Your prayers and our time together have blessed me beyond measure.

Thank you to our Temple Baptist church family. You have each touched our lives in different ways. We feel honored that so many of you were a part of our debt-free journey. I still remember so vividly the Sunday morning right after we became debt free when Pastor Randy pulled us aside to congratulate us on our accomplishment and encourage us as we moved forward with our journey. To have a church, and a pastor, that has so closely known and supported our journey has been amazing. This church has been the best church we could have ever asked for to start our life together as a couple. I do not have the words to possibly thank you for all the ways you have touched our family.

Finally, thank you to Dave Ramsey and the whole team at Ramsey Solutions. My husband read books by a number of different financial gurus before we began our debt-free journey. But, Dave, it was your book and your principals that really resounded with him. You inspired him to want something better for our family. Thank you to Dave and to the whole Ramsey Solutions team for giving us the tools to be gazelle intense. We would not have accomplished this journey – and we would not have this story to tell – without the help of your books, your programs, and your inspiration.

We are about to share 50 awesome money-saving tips with you, but before we dive into the tips themselves, let me share with you a little bit of our story – the story of our journey to become debt free.

our story

In December 2014, my husband and I got married. When I married my husband, I also married into a variety of debt including student loans, credit cards, and furniture notes. Now, luckily, my husband had recently had a 'come-to-Jesus moment' of sorts and knew just how deadly debt and money issues could be in a marriage. (Not-so-fun fact: Money fights are the number two reason for divorce.[1])

That come-to-Jesus moment happened when he graduated as a fifth-year senior from the private university we both attended. When he saw his student loan summary upon his graduation, he realized why it is that so many people live on the verge of being broke. He also realized that he wanted a better life for his family, a life where we didn't have to live paycheck to paycheck. Thus, he took full responsibility for his debt and began to take steps to conquer his payments.

Taking full responsibility meant that, before we were even married, my husband had begun reading practically any solid financial book that he could find. In fact, our last unmarried summer, he even purchased a book (*Smart Women Finish Rich* by David Bach) for me that focused on budgeting and preparing for retirement specifically for women.

So, when we were married in December 2014, thanks to financial experts such as Larry Winget, David Bach, and Dave Ramsey, my husband had quite a few financial principles under his belt. He had even started to implement a few of these principles on his own. Simply put, my husband hated his debt. He hated the reminder of his irresponsibility with money, and he wanted to get rid of that debt.

Even more, he wanted to provide the best future possible for me, the child I was carrying, and any possible children in the future (which turned from a possibility to a reality before I even began writing this book). Not only did he envision a future for his family that was free of debt, but he also saw a future that included an incredible retirement plan, school funding for our children, and, best of all, the power to give to others in amazing ways. We both wanted all of this, and because of our desire to use the money bestowed on us by God more wisely, we immediately began attacking these debts.

So, in December 2014, our journey to become debt free begun. When I use the term 'debt free,' I am including all of our debts except our mortgage. If you follow Dave Ramsey's Baby Steps[1], you know that paying off your primary home comes in a later step than the rest of your debt, as it is not considered consumer debt.

Now, when I began this story I listed the debts that I acquired upon marrying my husband. Unfortunately, the list of debts didn't stop there. We acquired more debts and financial setbacks as a couple, including the following:

Hospital bills.
We did not have the savings to cash flow the birth of our first daughter, so we paid off our hospital bill over the course of a few months. We were smart and had savings in place by the birth of our second child.

Contractor bills.
My husband bought a 1950's home just a couple months before we were married, and our home has required a few major construction projects in the last three years. Needless-to-say, we have learned some good lessons regarding contracts and using contractors, which we will share later in this book.

More student loans.
During the first year and a half of our debt-free journey, my husband was attending school to earn his Master's Degree in Business Administration, which he finished just before the birth of our second daughter. Dave Ramsey would definitely frown on us having acquired more student loan debt when we were already deep in debt. I will admit, we didn't quite follow the plan there, and if we were to do it all over again, we would *not* have done it that way! That said, on the flip side, because he was earning this graduate level degree, my husband was hired for a new position, his income increased, and he was home more often. Thus, it was a good decision for our family, but it cost us debt-free freedom for another year!

Our total debt, including all of the debts prior to our marriage and those acquired since our marriage, came in just under $97,000. It took us 26 months to pay off this debt. When we began our debt free journey, we had a household income of about $40,000, which increased to about $65,000 by the end of our journey. I say "household income" because, although I am a stay-at-home mom, I bring in some income by teaching piano and clarinet lessons, playing piano at a local church, and selling homemade items.

Now, I know you're probably running some quick math and figuring that those numbers don't quite add up. We had around $105,000 in earnings and $97,000 in debt. How does that work? Well, first of all, remember that it was slightly over two years, so it was a bit more than that quick total. Secondly, we sold many items to free up more cash. There was one time, in a two-week period, that I made $1,000 selling items we no longer used on our community's buy/sell Facebook page. Yes, $1,000 in just two weeks! Thirdly, we lived on just fifteen percent of our income. You heard me right, fifteen percent. We were able to do this – living on fifteen percent of our income and paying off our debt in just over two years – in large part thanks to Dave Ramsey, financial expert and talk show host of the Dave Ramsey radio show, a show dedicated to providing people with financial advice.

I don't say all of this to brag about what we have accomplished. Instead, my intention is to show you that it is possible. You aren't stuck, it's not too late, and any excuse you have is a house of cards. As Dave says, "Leave the cave, kill something, and drag it home." You can do this, too!

Thanks to Dave and his team, my husband and I learned about living on a budget, insurance of all types, taxes, buying/selling a home, retirement, college savings, the list goes on. These were truly the lessons on "adulting" that we needed!

So, in January 2015, as newlyweds we sat down together and slowly began to figure out our finances – we began to build our budget together. I say 'slowly' because it really was a slow process! It took time for us to figure out how much we needed in each category of our budget – time to figure out where we needed more and where we could cut costs. This process took months to perfect, but now we can practically do it in our sleep.

Each of the financial principles and cost cutting methods that we employed along the way took time, practice, and patience to implement. They often involved much research and cost comparison, as we considered whether each method would really save us money and if it was worth the time required to implement. They took dedication, diligence, and discipline. In order for our debt-free plan to work, we had to continually remind ourselves of our goals, and accept the sacrifice that it was going to take to get there.

With our debt-free goal constantly in the forefront of our minds, these (sometimes crazy and a bit excessive) cost cutting methods seemed, to us, not so crazy and highly important. And, best of all, they worked! These cost cutting methods and financial principles got us out of debt!

On March 1, 2017 (the month that my husband would turn 26 and I would turn 24) we made our very last student loan payment and paid off the remainder of our debt! We did this one month earlier than our previously set goal and six months earlier than the original goal we set when we began this process.

That morning when we pushed the submit button together and watched the last of those student loans disappear, with our two beautiful daughters sitting in our laps, may have been one of the best days of our life together! We were done, and we were free. I can't even put into words what a relief I felt. We were so invigorated by our financial success, knowing that we were free of all our debt, a lifestyle to which we vowed never to return.

Now, the goal of this book is not to educate you about budgets (although I will touch briefly on their importance) or to tell you the best way to invest for retirement. I am by no means a financial expert. So, I will leave those conversations for experts like Dave Ramsey and Chris Hogan. These men have plenty of awesome books, podcasts, and other resources that will guide you through these topics and provide you with the tools you need to succeed wherever you are in your financial journey.

I am a stay-at-home mom, or as my husband prefers to call me (very proudly might I add), a 'domestic engineer.' What I know is how to cut costs. Living on fifteen percent doesn't work if you don't pay attention to where your money is going. I know how to cut costs and how to aid your family in successfully accomplishing whatever financial goals you may have in your future. The goal of this book is to share with you the top 50 ways that we cut costs during our journey to become debt free.

So, grab your cup of coffee (If you're currently paying off your debt, that coffee had better be homemade. No $5.00 cups of Starbucks coffee for you!), sit back, and enjoy as we cover some of the most effective and most awesomely, crazy ways to cut costs.

chapter one
A Written Plan is Necessary

I am going to share tons of little tips and tricks for saving money throughout the course of this book. But, quite frankly, unless you have a budget and are dedicated to your budget (and, if you are married, I add that unless you communicate all of this with your spouse!), nothing else is going to work. You *must* have a budget.

If you are going to build a house, you need blueprints. If you are going to drive across the country, you need a map. If you are going to be financially successful, you NEED a budget!

Tip #1
Nothing Else Matters if You Don't Have a Budget

There is so much I could say about budgets. My husband and I have learned a lot about budgeting and communication during our debt-free journey, but I am going to touch on just a couple of things.

Don't be scared by budgets.
First of all, please do not let the word 'budget' scare you. So many people hear the word 'budget' and relate it to a negative thing. *It's not in the budget. We blew our budget. There is a budget deficit.*

Yet my husband and I always smile when we hear the word budget. You see, having a budget means that we are in control of our money. Because we are in control, our budget will always say whatever we want it to say. If we want it to have $200 set aside for eating out, then our budget will reflect that. Realistically, our budget said $0 for eating out while we getting out of debt. But that's what we *told* it to say.

Looking over our previous budgets (which I can do because my nerdy husband keeps our budgets on an Excel spreadsheet that dates back to the beginning of our marriage), it was fun to see how intense we got throughout this process. We didn't always live on fifteen percent of our income. When we began this process, we were budgeting our living expenses around 45 percent. However, the last six months or so we really cinched down scraping by on 13-15 percent. It wasn't much fun at the time (ok, it really was not fun at all), but we never have to do that again and *that* is pretty cool. Dave Ramsey says: "Live like no one else, so later, you can live and give like no one else."

Get on a budget!

Second of all, once you have gotten yourself comfortable with the word 'budget,' then get on a budget! More specifically, you need to use the zero based budgeting technique as taught by Dave Ramsey and many other financial experts. In this method of budgeting, you total the amount of household income (just the take-home pay, not your total income because you don't get to use the money that goes to pay taxes or Social Security). Then, write all of your expenses down for the month. Between money used to tithe, pay bills, buy necessary items, invest, etc., every penny should be accounted for. At the bottom of the budget should be ($0.00). Every penny gets an assignment, even those pennies being saved. In other words, no soldier without his marching orders. Dollars that don't get assignments will disappear. They will get spent without even a second thought. Side note: Some people get a little freaked when they are introduced to zero based budgeting. The most common misconception is that because there is $0.00 at the bottom of the budget, then you don't have any money left. Remember that your budget should include spending and saving, so you aren't spending everything. You are just designating each penny!

Be intentional with this. Don't just make the budget. Actually, stick to it. If you are new to budgeting, this may be hard. It is easy to fudge 'just this one time.' So, until you build self-discipline it might mean leaving your debit card at home. Or it may mean paying at the pump for awhile, so you aren't enticed by all of those yummy gas station snacks. When we started this journey, my husband would leave his debit cards at home and only carried a $20 bill for his budgeted spending amount. This was only until the self-discipline was built, of course.

If you have tried budgeting and can't seem to stick to it. Or if you are a budgeting 'newbie' and need some extra encouragement, here are a few tips to help you stay true to your budget:

Find an accountability partner.

Find someone to hold you accountable to your budget. If you are married, this would be your spouse! If you are single, you will want to find someone you trust who will encourage you to stick to your budget (tip...don't pick your friend who loves impulse buys and shopping sprees).

Whoever you choose for your accountability partner (a spouse, friend, family member, etc.), make sure to communicate openly and check in routinely with this person. That might mean a weekly budget check or maybe just communicating twice a month about how things are going.

Make a budget that works for you.

So many people are scared to make a budget because they are afraid they won't be able to have fun. Let me tell you...we just returned from a two-week vacation. We had lots of fun and we did the whole vacation on a budget! We knew this trip was coming, so we saved for the trip. The cost of the trip was included in our December and January budgets!

So, when you're making your budget, be sure to include the fun things you would like to do – a date night with your spouse, a trip to the big city, or a movie ticket and snacks!

Make it visual.

Your budget should be put in writing...either pen to paper or type it up on your computer! But, as a very visual person myself, sometimes I need something more that just the budget sheet.

For example, when we were paying off our debt, we made 'debt thermometers' that we hung on our fridge. Every time we made another payment, we shaded in our thermometer. The visual component was a great way to keep us focused on our goal!

Now, if you don't have debt, you can do the same thing for your savings. If you have a certain savings goal in mind – saving for a new washer, saving for an upcoming trip, or saving a certain amount for retirement this year – you can make a savings thermometer for that goal as well!

Whatever you can do to make your budget visual – whether you use an app that tracks it for you and gives you something to look at or you dedicate a whole wall in your home to your financial goal – do whatever it takes!

Use the cash envelope system.

When you use the cash envelope system, you withdraw cash for the different areas of your budget. Each budget category receives a different envelope. This system makes it really easy to track how much you have left in a specific budget area. In addition, you tend to spend less when you pay with cash. We don't 'feel' money the same way when we pay with a card. We just swipe that little piece of plastic and life goes on. When we pay with cash and we have to hand over a twenty or fifty-dollar bill, we really feel that being spent.

Now, you aren't going to withdraw cash for every budget area. My husband and I have all of our bills withdrawn automatically from our account, so obviously we do not withdraw cash to pay our bills. We typically withdraw cash for the following budget categories: groceries, Walmart (this is what we call our household products/hygiene products category of our budget), my husband's GEM money (gas, entertainment, and miscellaneous – his fun money), my GEM money, and any spending money we have budgeted for buying necessities for our girls. Our budget categories do change. For example, if we have designated money for buying holiday gifts or we are going on a trip, we may have additional budget areas that we need to pull out as cash.

The categories for which you decide to use the cash envelope system may differ from ours. It is an especially good idea to use cash for budget areas in which you tend to overspend. Cash will help you keep these areas in check and you will likely spend less!

Use an app to track your budget.
After my last budget tip, if you are still not sold on using cash, then please get a budgeting app like EveryDollar to help you track your spending. If you are using your debit card to pay for all of your different budget categories, it can take quite a bit of time to pull up your online bank statement, sort through all of your purchases, and calculate your remaining balance for each budget category.

A budgeting app will do all of this work for you! If you use an app such as EveryDollar, you will input your monthly budget. Then, if you link the app to your bank account, each time you make a purchase you can assign that purchase to a specific budget area. The app will then deduct the purchase from that category and show an easy visual breakdown of the remaining money in each budget category.

There are a number of budgeting apps on the market. Many of them cost a small fee (EveryDollar costs $99 per year.), but it is worth the fee if it helps you track and stick to your budget. You don't need to use the EveryDollar app, just be sure to find a budgeting app that works for you!

Get your budget in place BEFORE the month begins.
Each month, you will have a new budget. Chances are that many of your budget categories will remain the same each month. Your mortgage/rent, your phone bill, your garbage fees, and other expenses such as these should remain the same from month to month. However, other categories may change

each month. Your gas budget will fluctuate depending on how much you are traveling a given month. Your food budget will likely be higher if you have company coming to visit. Certain areas will change month by month, and you will need to give special consideration to these areas.

Each month, you will need to create a budget that will work for that particular month. Make sure you have this budget ready to go *before* the first of the month. If you get to the first of the month and don't have a budget ready to go, but you need to stop at the grocery store after work, you might be tempted to just make this quick trip and figure out the budget later. But, that night gets busy and you don't get around to doing the budget. Then, the next day you have to pick up a birthday treat for one of your coworkers, again thinking that you will get around to doing your budget.

This can carry on for a few days or even longer with no budget set in place. You haven't given your soldiers marching orders. Instead you are just spending "willy nilly," as my mom would say. This will *not* help you stick to your budget. Therefore, get your budget in place early, so you are ready to go when the month starts. Then, you won't be tempted to spend without having a plan in place.

Give yourself, and your spouse, grace.

Honestly, this is the most important tip I can give you when it comes to figuring out your budget. While budgeting is so important, it can be hard when you (and your spouse, if married) are first getting started. Chances are good that you *will* forget a thing or two in your first few months of budgeting. You will likely end up holding a few emergency budget meetings. And it will take you awhile to figure out what needs you have in each of your budget categories.

While budgeting can be messy at first, I promise it will get easier. (Keep in mind that it takes about 90 days to get good at budgeting.) If you give yourself, and your spouse, grace when you mess up and keep moving forward with your budgeting efforts, your budget will get easier and go much more smoothly with each passing month. You will likely find yourself spending less, saving more, making extra payments on your debt, and reaching your financial goals faster than you expected. Just don't forget, give yourself and your spouse grace.

There is so much more that could be said about budgets, but I would prefer that you read what the financial experts, like Dave Ramsey, have to say. If you are interested in learning more about the specifics of budgeting, visit Dave Ramsey's website and check out their free online tools to learn how to make a zero based budget, try out the EveryDollar budget app, access free budgeting forms, and so much more.

One last thing I will say…if my husband and I had not had a budget, I honestly do not think we would have achieved this financial goal of being debt free…or at least it would have taken way longer! Our budget was crucial to our success. It kept us focused on our goals; it kept us honest; and it kept us communicating about our finances. And it continues to keep us focused, honest, and communicating. Just because we have paid off our debt doesn't mean we are done budgeting. Goodness no! We are about to cash flow three years of law school for my husband, and we are going to need our budget to accomplish that goal too. Whether you are buried in debt or you have just made your first million, a budget is *always* a must.

So, if you are reading this book and you don't have a budget, please put down this book (if you are married, grab your partner) and get a budget before you read any further.

chapter two
Children Are Expensive!

**Note: If you do not yet have children, this section will likely bore you! So, skip ahead to page 51. However, if you have kids, you are expecting, you are trying to have kids, or you are planning on adopting or fostering, then read on. There's lots of good stuff here!

Let's face it – children are expensive. When we began our debt-free journey, we were already about six months pregnant with our first child. Just seventeen months after the birth of our first little girl, we brought home our second daughter. (And as we are getting closer to publishing this book, my stomach just keeps getting bigger and bigger. Yes, Baby #3 is on the way!) Our oldest daughter is only three, so while we don't fully understand the expenses of raising a house full of teenagers, we do know how very expensive the first few years can be for a family.

We get it – the hospital bills, doctor's appointments, diapers, wipes, clothes, milk, baby food – these things add up. Some costs simply can't be avoided. But, there are a number of ways that we were able to cut costs and save our family's budget from being dominated by the costs of raising children. If you are currently expecting or plan to be expecting soon, I want to take a moment to share something with you before we jump into our specific tips.

Like I mentioned before, when we brought our first little girl home from the hospital, we did not have enough savings to pay the medical bills. Rather, we paid them off over the course of a few months. When we found out we were expecting our second baby, we had about seven months to prepare for her arrival and we knew we wanted to be financially prepared this time.

Now, when we read that little digital word "Pregnant," we were in the middle of our debt-free journey. It was definitely not an ideal time to have big expenses coming our way. Right then, we made the decision to pause all additional debt payments. We continued paying the minimum payments on each of our debts. However, instead of paying extra on our debt, we put that money into savings – savings that were designated to pay our hospital bills. By the time our second daughter was born, we had more than $10,000 sitting in that savings account.

We paid our hospital bills, which thankfully came out to be significantly less than $10,000. After we had paid our hospital bills, we took the rest of those savings and made a large payment on our debt. That felt good! We had paid all our hospital bills upfront *and* we made a big dent in our debt as well!

So, if you are expecting or hope to be expecting very soon, here's my question for you: Do you know the average cost of having a baby? According to the Kaiser Family Foundation, "The average bill for doctors' fees and hospital charges runs around $9,700 for a normal delivery and roughly $12,500 for a cesarean section."[1] These numbers only include the labor and delivery. They do not include all of the prenatal visits also necessary during pregnancy. Be aware that the costs will vary based on a number of factors including the mother's insurance coverage, the baby's insurance coverage, the number of days spent in the hospital, and the interventions needed for mom and baby. (Please don't let these numbers scare you away from ever having kids. We have lots of tips to help you prepare for and reduce the costs of raising kids, so just keep on reading!)

If you are currently expecting a baby or hope to soon be expecting, make it your mission to save as much as you can up to $10,000 before your baby arrives. (Side note: If you are preparing for an adoption, you will also need to make it your mission to save for your child. I can't speak specifically to the amount you should plan for adoption as we have never adopted, but I know it can be expensive!) That means, if you are in the middle of a debt-free journey, you will likely need to pause additional payments.

Once you have paid your hospital bills and both mom and baby are healthy at home, take any leftover 'baby savings' and apply it to your debt (or if you are not in a debt-free journey, apply that remaining savings to one of your other financial goals).

Blessings on your pregnancy (or on your upcoming adoption)! I hope that we can help you financially prepare for your baby's arrival so that when your little bundle arrives you can focus on soaking up newborn snuggles instead of worrying about how to pay the bills.

I am going to take the next few pages to share some of our most effective cost cutting methods in the baby/kid section of our budget. I hope these tips give you lots of tools to help you reduce the costs of raising a kid. However, as you read, keep in mind that every family has different expenses. Some families use daycare, some don't. Some use disposable diapers, some use cloth. If you are looking for a more precise estimate of what it will cost *your* family to raise a child, visit the Baby Center website and use their First-Year Baby Costs Calculator.[2] This will help you think through the first year expenses and calculate an estimated total cost. Having this estimate will help you make a budget and put savings in place that are prepared for your family's needs.

Tip #2

Cloth Diapers and Cloth Wipes

Did you know that the average child will use more than 2,700 diapers in the first year alone? According to Investopedia[3], this can add up to more than $540 per year. This total is calculated based on an average price of $0.20 per disposable diaper. The cost of diapers will vary based on brand. If you use name-brand or special eco-friendly or hypoallergenic disposable diapers, you can expect to pay considerably more than this. And don't forget the wipes, which according to Investopedia, cost about $20 per month, or $240 per year.

All of these numbers mean that even if your child is potty trained by three years old, you have already spent about $2,340 on disposable diapers and wipes. And, think about the pounds and pounds of diaper garbage we put in our landfills. In addition to saving money, I'm pretty passionate about saving our Earth in any way that we can!

Wouldn't you love if you could spend less on diapers? Well, the good news is that you can! Cloth diapers are a very economically and environmentally friendly diapering option. Before we continue, please be aware that many states do not allow the use of cloth diapers in daycares, so be sure to check your state's policies before making a decision about how to diaper your child. When it comes to cloth diapers, it is hard to calculate the average cost to diaper a child as there are so many different brands/styles of diapers and different brands of detergents, both of which vary largely in price. However, when you consider disposable versus cloth, the upfront cost of cloth is more, but over time cloth always saves! We have spent less than $400 on cloth diapers and wipes for our children. Another perk of cloth diapering is that these diapers can be reused for a number of children!

Before the birth of our first daughter, we were blessed with lots of hand-me-down cloth diapers from my husband's sister, and a couple of cheap collections of cloth diapers acquired through garage sales. Thus, without spending much (less than $50 for quite a collection of diapers!), we were able to try a bunch of different brands and styles of cloth diapers. And, don't worry, it is perfectly fine to use second hand cloth diapers! Just give them a good washing before using them on your child.

Thanks to our random collection of cloth diapers, it didn't take long before we had settled on our favorite brand and style of diaper – the bumGenius Freetime. At the time this book was published, our favorite brand of diaper was retailing for about $19.95, give or take a few dollars depending on the print of the material used for the cloth diaper. Yes, that's $19.95 plus tax for *one diaper*!

While the bumGenius Freetime is a high-quality diaper, we still were not quite ready to spend that much per diaper. So, I started researching, and I found that there are ways to get high-quality (higher cost) cloth diapers at lower prices. Here are a few things to check if you are considering buying cloth diapers.

CottonBabies.com

Cotton Babies is the leading retailer of cloth diapers worldwide. This company is dedicated to anything and everything you could possibly need to cloth diaper your baby. They also offer a number of other baby products such as baby carriers, clothing, toys, baby gear, and much more. However, we are going to focus on their awesome cloth diaper deals! There are a few ways to score cheaper cloth diapers from Cotton Babies.

Buy in bulk.

Cotton Babies offers diaper packages, where you can buy a 6, 12, or 24-pack of cloth diapers. The larger package you purchase, the bigger the discount you receive. In other words, you are rewarded for buying in bulk! You can save quite a bit per diaper when you buy a 24-pack of cloth diapers.

Shop their online sales.

Cotton Babies also has a sale page on their website, where they offer certain styles of cloth diapers at much lower prices. For instance, you might find a bumGenius Littles (the newborn cloth diaper created by bumGenius) for $12.95 instead of $17.95. Or you might find a bumGenius Elemental for $19.95 instead of $24.95.

Buy used cloth diapers.

You can also buy used cloth diapers from Cotton Babies, as a part of their Growing Up in Cloth program. According to the official Cotton Babies website, "Our Growing Up in Cloth program was designed for economically minded parents who love cloth diapers! When your baby outgrows your cloth diapers, you may be able to trade them in for credit at Cotton Babies!"[4] Cotton Babies then re-sells these used cloth diapers for discounted prices. If you are interested in buying lower-cost cloth diapers or selling your used cloth diapers, check out the Cotton Babies website for more information.

Buy diapers on the Seconds Sale.

Finally, Cotton Babies has a Seconds Sale page. According to their website, "The products included in this category are second quality. Issues with these cloth diapers may be cosmetic (slightly uneven seams, dirt mark, small snags near the snaps, mis-printed fabric, etc.) or mild imperfections in the finishing. While finishing wasn't completely perfect, these diapers have been carefully inspected and they are definitely a saleable product."[5] And these diapers come at great prices. For example, you could score a bumGenius Freetime diaper for just $14.50 when they typically retail on Cotton Babies for about $19.95-21.95.

Do not hesitate to check out the official Cotton Babies website. In addition to offering better cloth diaper prices, they also offer all kinds of cloth diapering expertise. A full listing of their products and services can be found at http://www.cottonbabies.com.

Buy Buy Baby

When we fell in love with the bumGenius Freetime diaper, we actually purchased many of our diapers from Buy Buy Baby, a subsidiary of Bed, Bath, and Beyond. This store sells a few different brands of cloth diapers, including our favorite, the bumGenius Freetime. Every so often, Buy Buy Baby puts their bumGenius diapers on sale. Most times, the on-sale diapers aren't the 'cool' prints, but the lower price is so worth it!

However, that's not all! Bed, Bath, and Beyond sends me at least one coupon per month. These coupons are usually for 20 percent off of one item or $5 off a purchase of $15 or more. I was allowed to stack these coupons if I was buying a number of cloth diapers. By waiting for a sale on cloth diapers and stacking coupons, I was able to buy most of our bumGenius Freetime cloth diapers for just about $12! That's not bad, if you ask me, especially when you consider what disposable diapers would cost!

Cloth Wipes

In addition to using cloth diapers, we also use cloth wipes. You can buy cloth wipes. However, I enjoy sewing so I made our cloth wipes. I purchased a bunch of baby terry cloth towels from the thrift store. Using those towels and a few super thin flannel receiving blankets I had at home, I sewed some double-layer cloth wipes. I created wipes that were terry cloth on one side and flannel on the other side. I have since created additional cloth wipes because we use them for more than just bottoms. We love them for wiping little hands and faces and cleaning up spills around the house.

There are lots of different methods for making cloth wipes, and not all of them involve sewing. If you are interested in making your own cloth wipes, conduct a quick Google search. Trust me, there are plenty of mom blogs on the Internet with great cloth wipe making tutorials!

In total, we spent less than $400 on cloth diapers and cloth wipes. We use disposables many times when we travel, as it keeps things simpler, but we have still spent considerably less than $2,340 diapering our first child. In addition, that $400 worth of cloth diapers is now being used on our second child. We purchased a few more cloth diapers with our second child, as I found a stash of practically new BumGenius Freetime diapers being sold very cheaply – less than $10 per diaper! (So, we have actually spent about $500 on cloth diapers total.) This purchase expanded our stash just a bit, which helped as we had two children in diapers for a little while.

Keep in mind that these are just some of *my* tips regarding cloth diapering. There are so many different brands and styles of cloth diapers, and each person has to find one that works for their child(ren). I have quite a few mom friends who cloth diaper. Many of these moms also love BumGenius diapers. However, some of them have other cloth diaper brands (such as Thirsties, Grovia, and Alva) they prefer. So, check out websites and mom blogs. Do your research, try different diaper brands and styles, and figure out what works best for your child(ren).

Coupons for Disposable Diapers

If you decide you aren't up for cloth diapering or maybe your child spends enough time in daycare that cloth diapering simply isn't worth it, then this next section is for you! Even though we cloth diaper, we are not completely out of touch with disposable diapers and wipes since we use these conveniences when we travel. So, read on because I have a few tricks up my sleeve!

Use generic brand diapers.

First, try the generic brand! The generic brand diapers offered at most stores are typically quite a bit cheaper than Pampers, Huggies, or even Luvs diapers. We use the generic brand wipes, but we were unable to use the generic brand diapers as they gave our little girl a rash. However, if your child has no issues with the generic diapers, go for it! We have many friends who have successfully used generic diapers on their children.

Sign up for rewards programs.

Second, if generic brand diapers don't work for your child, then find a name brand diaper that works and take part in their rewards program. Like I mentioned before, the generic brand diapers don't work for us. So, when we travel and need disposable diapers, we buy either Pampers or Luvs diapers.

Pampers offers a rewards program called Pampers Rewards. It is exactly what it sounds…you are rewarded for buying Pampers diapers! When you buy Pampers diapers, there is a rewards code on the packaging. You make an account with Pampers Rewards, enter that code online, and earn points which can be used to redeem a number of different rewards. You won't necessarily get money back, and you won't save any money upfront, but you will earn access to some fun rewards!

Whatever diaper company you choose to buy from, be sure to check out their website to see if they offer any coupons or rewards programs. In addition to the programs highlighted above, Luvs and GoodNites diapers both currently offer coupons on their websites. It is always a great idea to check diaper manufacturer websites for coupons.

Use coupons/rebates when buying diapers and wipes.
Finally, using printed coupons, coupon apps, or rebate apps can help you save money on diapers and wipes.

One great place to look for diaper and wipe coupons is on www.coupons.com or the Coupons.com app. This website and app offer coupons for countless food, baby, household, and hygiene items. You choose which coupons you want to use, install their coupon printing program, and print the coupons right from your computer. Or, if you are using their app, you can redeem many of their coupon offers right from your phone.

Also be sure to check out rebate apps, such as Ibotta or Flipp, which I will discuss in more detail later in this book. When you use these apps you earn cash back on certain purchases. They often have rebates for both disposable diapers and wipes.

When using coupons and rebates, you can even 'stack' offers. Meaning, if the Coupons app and the Ibotta app are offering deals on Luvs diapers, you can use both offers and save even more on your diapers!

There are so many ways to save money on diapers. Whether you choose to use cloth diapers or shop name-brand disposable diapers with a fist full of coupons, you can cut costs in this budget area for sure!

Tip #3

Breastfeed...or Get Lots of Formula Coupons!

Once again, let's talk about the yearly costs for a baby. Do you know the average cost to formula feed a baby for one year? According to The Simple Dollar, "over the first year of life, average formula to feed an average baby costs $1,733.75."[6] Breaking down that total, we find that is just $144.48 per month spent on formula. Ok. In our budget, that wouldn't classify as a *'just.'* That's more than half of my typical grocery budget for a month. On the other hand, breastfeeding an infant for one year costs nothing!

With both of our girls, I chose to breastfeed. I had a variety of reasons for choosing to breastfeed – the cost efficiency was just one of the perks! Now, I understand that breastfeeding isn't feasible for everyone. Some women struggle with milk production. Some women are working (although, I know many working moms who have been very successful with pumping at work...so don't give up hope if you are in this category!). However, because everyone is different and I know that not every mom can breastfeed, I am going to highlight a few different options that will help you cut the cost of feeding your infant.

As I stated before, breastfeeding is the most cost-effective option, coming in at $0 per year. I mean, you have to make sure that, as the mom, you have enough to eat and drink, but there are no additional costs for your milk beyond feeding yourself. If you wish to pump and bottle feed, there will be the costs of a pump, bottles, and breast milk storage bags. However, these items will still cost significantly less than formula.

One last quick tip for breastfeeding mommas...if you decide that you want to have a breast pump, check with your medical insurance company about whether or not they will cover the cost of a breast pump. Some medical insurance companies will pay for your breast pump if your doctor writes you a prescription for a breast pump. Before the birth of our first daughter, I was able to get a very nice Medela breast pump for free thanks to my insurance policy.

Now, if you decide to forgo breastfeeding and opt to formula feed your infant instead, I have a few tips to help make this option much more cost-effective for you!

Request free samples.

First of all, many formula companies will send you free samples when you are expecting. If you put in your name, mailing information, and baby's due date, they will send you a free sample or two in the mail. The samples are a pretty good size – we are talking entire cans of formula! I received samples from both Gerber and Similac with each of my pregnancies. Tip: Even if you primarily breastfeed, it's always nice to have formula available for backup…trust me.

In addition, typically hospitals send home a goodie bag with new infants that has all kind of helpful baby information (information on local programs, tips for baby care, and so on) along with lots of great samples. My goody bags have included a Avent bottle, a can of formula, and other great samples! So, to recap…get all of the formula samples that you possibly can!

Sign up for rewards/coupon programs.

Second, some formula companies allow you to sign up for their rewards/coupon programs. I receive coupons from both Similac and Enfamil. Again, it's nice to have backup, even if you are breastfeeding.

We ended up formula feeding our first daughter for about one month before she turned one. We used Similac so I can speak to how their coupon program works. Every month or so, they send out a mailing with anywhere from one to three coupons. Typically, the coupons start at $5 off one container of Similac formula. As you use coupons, your account builds and you are sent coupons worth more – sometimes upwards of $15-18 off one container of Similac.

Like I mentioned, Similac is not the only company that offers coupons. Enfamil has a similar program. In addition, Gerber offers certain promotions to anyone who signs up for MyGerber.

Use a rebate app to earn cash back.
Third, later in this book, I will discuss in detail a rebate app called Ibotta. If you are formula feeding your baby, I encourage you to check out this app! Ibotta typically offers some formula rebates. In fact, I was just searching on Ibotta earlier this week, and found that they currently have rebates for a number of different Similac and Enfamil formulas. The rebates ranged from $2.50 to $5.00 cash back per container of formula.

Whether you decide to breastfeed or formula feed, there are a number of options to save money while still ensuring that your baby is well fed. Take a moment to look into these options…it could save you more than $1,700 in just one year!

**Investment Opportunity:* Let's say that you decide to breastfeed your child. Instead of spending $1,700 on formula for the first year, you invest that money in a money market account that makes, on average, ten percent annually. By the time your child goes to school eighteen years later, they will have $9,451.86 for schooling…from just one year's worth of investing!

Tip #4
Buy the Cheapest Milk

After year one, your child will likely switch from breast milk or formula to whole milk. Every parent who has a little one currently in the 'whole milk stage,' or has had kids in that stage previously knows that whole milk is *not* cheap. In fact, milk in general is not cheap.

When I first began writing this book, whole milk was about $0.25 more per gallon than two percent or skim milk. However, milk prices have gone up in the past year. Now, every kind of milk at Walmart costs $3.58 per gallon. Side note, milk prices may vary greatly by location! My mom lives in a more rural area of our state, so a gallon of whole milk would cost her more than $4.00. Milk prices will vary by state as well because different states have different state minimums. One of our neighboring states has a *much* lower milk minimum, so if we are headed to do shopping in that state, you can be sure we will be buying milk while we are there! Thus, you may find that milk in your area is more expensive than the numbers I am sharing, or you may find it's much cheaper. Regardless, my numbers will provide a good illustration for this tip.

Our younger daughter is still currently in the 'whole milk stage,' while our older daughter has moved on to drinking lower fat milk! By themselves, our girls each drink about one gallon of milk every 9-11 days or so. That means that every pay period (remember, my husband and I budget on a bi-weekly basis), I have to buy about two gallons of whole milk and two gallons of lower fat milk to have enough milk for our entire family. Of course, this increases if we end up with company.

So, let's get down to the nitty gritty prices. Milk prices have been steadily on the rise where we live. The store brand milk at Walmart is usually about $3.58 per gallon of milk. That means, for two weeks, I will spend at least $14.32 on milk. During the most intense stages of paying off our debt, our grocery budget was usually only $75-$100 for a two-week period. That means, our milk alone was 14-19% of our total grocery budget.

Now, I know that some of you reading this are thinking…man, I wish I had numbers like hers! If you are the mom of four teenage boys, I can't even imagine how much milk must be purchased in a two-week period for your household! Thus, I make my point even more strongly. It is worth it to search your community to find the lowest milk price.

When prices continued to climb at Walmart (where milk had always been the lowest for us), we began to search our community to see if we could find a cheaper option for milk…and sure enough, we found it! It wasn't at all where we guessed we would find it. We discovered the cheapest milk was at the hardware store.

You see, at the hardware store, we could get a gallon of whole milk for about 30 cents less. It's not a lot cheaper, but over time it's enough to make a difference on our budget. Now, if buying the cheapest milk means that you have to drive twenty miles out of your way, then it may not be worth your time and your gas money. You need to weigh the costs of all factors involved before driving around town to buy the cheapest milk.

Be aware that where you find the cheapest milk may change over time. While I mentioned above that we had found milk to be cheapest at the hardware store, after quite a few months we noticed the prices had started to increase. Due to a significant change in the hardware store price, Walmart was once again the cheapest option. Always be aware of changing prices and check all of your options so that you can get the best price for your product!

The example here was focused on milk, but this can be done for any product. If there are multiple grocery stores in your area, take a notebook with you and jot down prices for the things you commonly use such as milk, eggs, cheese, coffee, toilet paper, etc. Compare prices and find the best spot for you to do your shopping. These price differences may seem miniscule, but every little bit helps and will add to your financial success.

After three years of shopping for my family, I now know the sales well enough that I can glance at my list and know exactly where I am going to shop. With two little girls, I don't want to be running to every grocery store in town to score different deals, so I am going to choose the store where I will get the best possible deals on the majority of my items. For example, if I am in need of a number of gluten free items, I am likely going to shop at Walmart, as they tend to have the lowest prices in town on gluten free products. However, if I am in need of a lot of produce, I am more likely to shop at Cashwise – one of the grocery stores in our town and the one that typically has the best produce prices.

I decided to do a little cost comparison of common products our family uses at a few different stores. Check out my findings in the table below.

Item	Grocery Store	Walmart	Sam's Club
1% Milk	$3.09/gal.	$2.77/gal.	$2.89/gal.
Chobani Greek Yogurt	$0.17/oz.	$0.16/oz.	$0.12/oz.
On the Border Corn Chips	$0.23/oz.	$0.17/oz.	$0.14/oz.
Tide Powder Laundry Detergent	$0.18/oz.	$0.13/oz.	$0.12/oz.
Total Spent	**$38.41**	**$29.54**	**$26.41**

When you look at the prices per ounce listed in this table, the difference seems miniscule – it's just pennies. But, look at the total spent at each store buying *just* these four products. There was a $12 difference between the highest total, at a local grocery store, and the lowest total, at Sam's Club. A $12 difference on a purchase of just four products! Think how much greater of a difference there would be if your cart had twenty or more items filling it. This is a perfect example of why it pay to shop around and really know your prices!

Over time, you too will learn where to find the best prices to match the needs of your household! Just be sure to do some serious comparison-shopping, especially for those products that you purchase on a weekly basis.

**Disclaimer:* Keep in mind that when I discuss product prices (especially for food items) in this book, they may be quite different from the prices in the store where you shop. Prices largely vary based on where you live and the stores you have available to shop. For example, I can buy a gallon of milk for about $3.24 at Walmart in one North Dakota town. In another ND town just 2.5 hours away but slightly bigger, I can easily get a gallon of milk for under $3.00 at Walmart. However, if I go visit my mom in a rural ND town (where there is only a local grocery store), I would pay over $4.00 for a gallon of milk.

Tip #5

Make Your Own Baby Food

I don't know the cost of baby food where you live, but for us a two-pack of Gerber baby food costs about $2.00. Now, a two-pack of baby food would have lasted our first little girl quite a few meals, but our second (who ate more like the average baby) would have plowed through one container of food per meal or more. That gets expensive fast. That's at least $1.00 per meal...not including all the other baby snacks she also munched throughout the day.

Comparatively, bananas usually cost us about $0.59 per pound or less. That means I can get a whole bunch of bananas for just a couple of dollars! By mixing a banana or two with some breast milk and blending, I can make enough food for multiple feedings, and I will have spent a lot less! In addition, I have total control over what my baby is consuming, so no added preservatives! Side note: If you aren't breastfeeding, just substitute formula instead. You can also 'bulk up' baby food using a baby cereal, such as rice cereal or oatmeal.

If you are going to make your own baby food, you will need to have a kitchen tool that is capable of pureeing food. If you have a blender or a food processor, you are good to go! If you don't have a kitchen tool ready for the job, I will put in a good word for the Baby Bullet.

The Baby Bullet is not cheap. It usually retails for about $59.99. Luckily, we received ours as a baby gift because I don't honestly think we would have spent that money on our own. So, if you have a baby registry, add the Baby Bullet to your registry, and you may be blessed by a family member like we were!

Aside from the price, I love the Baby Bullet. It comes with a number of accessories, including two different size containers and lids for pureeing food, storage containers that make for easy freezing, a spatula, and a cookbook dedicated to everything you could possibly need to know about baby food!

I also love the small size of the baby bullet. It makes it easy to travel and make food on the go! In addition, I don't have to make our *entire* Ninja blender dirty when I want to puree a meal for our daughter. The clean up with the Baby Bullet is much simpler.

Do not feel obligated to purchase a $60 Baby Bullet. Find any kitchen tool that will puree food (a blender, food processor, etc.), do some research on Google to find tips and recipes for making your own baby food, and just get started! This won't take a lot of additional time in your day, and it is certain to be a money-saver!

Tip #6
Avoid Buying Baby Clothes and Toys

If you have a family, chances are you have some aunts that absolutely love buying baby and kids clothes or some grandparents who look forward to getting that little grandson or granddaughter a new toy. Embrace these gifts!

When we were expecting our first daughter, I purchased baby clothes from thrift stores and sleepers from the great Carter's fleece sleeper sale. I bought some onesies, pants, cotton sleepers, and fleece sleepers. It was a nice little collection, but in the grand scheme of things, it was definitely not enough clothes to outfit a baby for the entire first year.

Well, thanks to all of our family and friends, I didn't actually have to buy any clothes for our daughter until she was about two years old. We were blessed with clothes given as birthday and Christmas presents, 'just because' packages, and hand-me-downs from friends.

When it came to toys, I didn't buy any toys before the birth of our first child. And in actuality, your child doesn't need many toys for the first year of their life. A small basket of toys will more than suffice! Once again, we were given plenty of toys for our baby, and for her first birthday, she received a number of new toys!

I have learned that it never hurts to give family and friends gift ideas if they are planning on surprising your little one for his or her birthday or for Christmas. If there is a particular size or season of clothes that your baby needs or a toy that you think would match his or her developmental stage, let your family and friends know!

I remember, after we had our first daughter, my dad's family hosted a baby shower for us. They waited with the shower until after the birth, so they could all meet the baby and get plenty of baby snuggles. My dad had asked me prior to the baby shower what things we could use. We were so well outfitted with most baby items, even clothes. However, the clothes we had really only covered our little girl through the first twelve months. So, I suggested to my dad that he buy clothing sizes that would fit our little girl after the first year. This was one reason we were able to go two years before buying kid clothes.

Another way to avoid spending money on baby clothes is by borrowing baby clothes from others in your community! Babies grow so quickly that many outfits are only worn for a few months before being packed away in the closet. If you just ask, you will likely find that fellow moms are more than happy to share their child's clothes and free up some closet space. Just be sure to mark the tags with the initials of who the clothes belong to so that you can be sure to return them to the correct person!

With all of the advertising that we see every day on social media, it is easy to find yourself purchasing another cute baby outfit off of Etsy, or the latest water table for your kids to play in this summer. Be aware of this advertising! Do not get caught up in the belief that your child *needs* these items. Make sure that your child has the clothing items that they need. Aside from that, don't splurge on unnecessary clothes and toys. While it may be difficult to not splurge on your cute little kids, they will thank you later when you are able to help them pay for college. It is worth the sacrifice now.

Tip #7
Shop Thrift Stores

If you find yourself in a bind and your children are needing clothes (like I mentioned before, make sure that your kids have the clothes they need), then head to your local thrift or consignment stores!

I, personally, don't see any reason to spend full price on kids' clothes. Kids end up with food, dirt, and poop all over their clothes! Why pay full price for something that could very well end up stained with spaghetti or tattered with holes in the knees?

To give you a little idea about just how far your money can go when you shop thrift stores, here is a story about a thrifting experience of mine.

I needed to do some shopping for our toddler. She was a long, skinny two-year-old (at the time); and it seemed that every pair of pants she had was starting to look more like capris. While she still had some bigger hand-me-downs in the closet, they were all summer clothes – shorts, tank tops, and so on. She was in desperate need of pants and long sleeve shirts to wear until the warmer weather came. So, I set out with a budget of $35.

For that $35, I was able to get the following items (all items were in quite good condition, some even in new condition):

~ 2 fleece sleepers (Carter's brand)
~ 1 pair of corduroy pants
~ 7 pair of jeans (including brands like Oshkosh and Old Navy)
~ 1 long-sleeved fleece jacket (Carter's brand again)
~ 2 long sleeved shirts (one Carter's brand, one Old Navy brand)

Assuming I didn't forget anything, that is thirteen items for just

$35. Do some quick math and you will find that I spent about $2.70 per item. Wow!

Now, there are times that our thrift and consignment stores don't have a very good selection of kids clothes. In those cases, I usually head to one of the bigger cities near us and check their thrift stores, or shop garage sales in my area. I recently had a great day of shopping where I visited one garage sale and one thrift store (the store was having a big sale). I walked away with 51 items including one brand new winter coat, two brand new pairs of winter boots, and multiple brand new clothing items. And…the best part…I only spent $87. That's just $1.67 per item! I am still feeling excited from this trip!

However, if you're having trouble finding used clothing options, or you have a special occasion and want something new, I have a couple other tips that can help you save money on kids and baby clothes at non-thrift stores.

Shop the baby and kid sections at Walmart.

It seems that our local Wal-Mart is always marking down their baby and kids' clothes. Just recently, I scored a pair of pajamas for my toddler for just $1, and matching dresses for the girls for $3 each. Now, I will admit, the pajamas are definitely not as good quality at my daughter's Carter's brand pajamas, but for $1 I was willing to sacrifice a little quality!

Watch for sales and end-of-season clearance events.

Most stores offer great prices on clothes at the end of the season. Meaning, when winter is finishing and spring begins to bud, all of the winter clothes are marked down – sometimes quite significantly. If you can plan ahead and buy your child's clothes for next winter during this end-of-season clearance, you will definitely save some money!

Additionally, many stores have sales that you can practically bank on. For instance, let's take the store Carter's. I shopped this baby and kids' clothing store when I was pregnant with our first child. You can pretty much bank on Carter's running an awesome fleece sleeper sale at least a few times every year!

I hit up Carter's fleece sleeper sale before our first was born and bought almost all of the fleece sleepers we needed for the first twelve months; and I didn't spend more than $6 on any sleeper. Some were even less! But, the fleece sleeper sale is not Carter's only sale. Every so often they run a 50 percent off sale that applies to almost everything in their store, and they have great clearance racks as well!

Join rewards programs.

Many stores offer rewards cards or allow you to sign up for their rewards programs. Now, I am NOT referring to store credit cards. Steer clear of those! Having a store credit card often encourages you to spend money that you don't have to spend. What I am talking about are simple rewards programs where the store tracks your purchases, both online and in-store, and offers you free money to spend in their store after you spend a certain amount.

For example, The Children's Place keeps track of the money you spend. Once you spend $100, you receive a $5 reward to spend on your next purchase. The Children's Place also often runs promotions where you get $10 for every $20 that you spend. That means you can earn more than just one $10 coupon. For example, if you spend $80, you will earn four $10 coupons. These $10 coupons can be spent on a future purchase from The Children's Place.

Now, the kicker with this promotion is that you have to then spend at least $20 on your next purchase to use a $10 off coupon. When you use a store's rewards program, be aware of the fine print. These programs can encourage you to spend more than you need. But, they also can be used to your advantage. If your child really needs some new clothes and you are able to place a couple orders, using coupons from the first order on the second order, you will pay less for those clothes!

Make it yourself.
While this tip doesn't necessarily relate to buying children's clothing from a store, it is still a great money saving option! Whether you are handy with a sewing machine or not, there are lots of DIY patterns to make easy, adorable clothes for your kids. Obviously, I've had more experience making little girls clothes, so I can confidently say that a pillowcase dress is a really simple creation (just a couple of straight seams). If you conduct a quick Google or Pinterest search, you will find plenty of free patterns for sewing kids' clothes. And, for all of you non-sewing people, I've seen plenty of pins on Pinterest for easy no-sew repurposed t-shirt dresses for little girls! So, get searching! There are many methods to make kids clothes without ever touching a sewing machine.

Why would I suggest to make it yourself? Well, while this will take some of your time, making your own clothes can be a cheaper option. Shop fabric store clearance racks and thrift stores to find material, or repurpose some of your old clothes. With such a little cost out of pocket for the supplies, you can afford to get creative and try your hand at making clothes for your kids!

When it comes to buying clothes for your kids, nothing beats thrift store and garage sale prices. But however you decide to save on baby and kids clothes, just be sure you are never paying full price. It simply doesn't pay!

Tip #8

Use Coupons or Watch for Sales on Big Ticket Items

What is one of the most expensive items we have purchased for our children? You probably guessed it...yes, car seats. We likely could have spent a bit less than we have on car seats, but we are particular about the brand of car seats we buy as we want our children riding in the very safest option! That being said, we have found other ways to reduce the costs of these car seats.

Here are a couple of things to consider when buying those 'big ticket' kids' items.

Store Coupons

Do you have a store that sells the necessary item and also offers coupons? We do! We have two large cities, each about 90 miles from where we live, that we visit to buy these bigger ticket items. Both cities have the store Buy Buy Baby (a subsidiary of Bed, Bath, and Beyond). At least once a month, I receive a sales flyer from Bed, Bath, and Beyond with a coupon or two. The coupon offers vary, but include promotions such as 20 percent off of one item or $5 off a purchase of $15 or more. These coupons are eligible for in-store use only.

I am also a part of Buy Buy Baby's email list, so I receive coupon offers via email as well. These offers are eligible for either in-store or online use, so I can use them to place an order for something not available in the store. If you spend more than $50 online, you also receive free shipping. With all of our car seat purchases, we have been able to use a 20 percent off of one item coupon. Both of our daughters currently use a convertible car seat that sells for about $300 plus tax, so by using a 20 percent off coupon, we saved around $60. We also used a 20 percent off coupon to buy our infant seat and stroller travel system. Again, we saved around $60 on this system.

Check out the stores that you frequent and sign up to receive coupons in the mail or via email. In addition, downloading a store's app or following a store's Facebook page are great ways to get your hands on more store coupons!

Rotating Sales

Most stores rotate sale items, so if you watch the sales carefully, your item may come up for sale. That's why it pays to plan ahead! I actually received an email the other day from Target. They were offering that a certain percentage off of your child's next car seat if you traded in their old car seat. Side note: While it does pay to plan ahead and take advantage of sales, be sure to consider expiration dates on a car seat before making a purchase. If a car seat will only be good for six years and it's going to sit in your child's closet for two years before they begin using it, wait for a sale that is closer to the time that your child will use that particular car seat.

Black Friday or Cyber Monday Deals

Many times stores offer some incredible prices on baby and kids' items during Black Friday and Cyber Monday sales. If you are able to find a good sale on the item you need during one of these sales, buy it then.

This past year I had to purchase a new car seat for our youngest daughter. She had outgrown her infant seat and it was time to buy her a convertible car seat. Now, as I previously explained, I purchased her seat from Buy Buy Baby using a 20 percent off coupon, saving our family around $60. I had researched prices and that was the best option; and I felt pretty good about saving $60.

Well, about a month later, Black Friday rolled around and I was perusing the flyer for a local baby and kids' items store. I just so happened to stumble on the same brand convertible car seat I had purchased for our daughter. Only thanks to the Black Friday sale, this seat was being sold for about $40 less than what I had paid for our daughter's seat *and* it was the newest model where the lining zips off making it super easy to wash! Let's just say I felt a little crummy about missing that sale. Unfortunately, I don't have a crystal ball that shows me all of the future sales, although that would be nice!

So, my advice for you is this, if Black Friday is around the corner and your purchase can wait, do so. You might find a better deal. If it can't wait, find the best deal possible using store coupons and/or online coupon codes.

Purchase from the Manufacturer's Website
Many manufacturers will offer coupons or special promotions on their websites. Friends of ours recently purchased a new car seat for their daughter. They decided to purchase that car seat straight from the manufacturer website; and they were just able to save $90 a promotion the manufacturer was offering. So, before settling on a price, be sure to check the manufacturer's website!

Just remember, you need to plan ahead with your budget when purchasing bigger ticket baby and kids' items. Research the item and find an estimated price (including the item's price, tax on the item, and approximate shipping costs). Then, figure out how much time you have before you will need to purchase the item. From there, you can determine how much you will need to save per week. For example, let's say you are saving to purchase your child's next car seat, which will cost about $250. You have six months until you plan on making this purchase. Thus, in order to save $250 over six months, you will need to save about $42 per month.

Most times, bigger ticket kids' items do not come suddenly. If you are expecting, you know you will need to save for a crib, a car seat, and a stroller (along with lots of smaller items). If you have a baby, you know that in a matter of months, you will need the next size car seat for your child. Thus, plan ahead. Prepare your budget so you can save for bigger ticket items. Then, if at all possible, buy these items on sale or use a store coupon and/or online coupon code to save money!

Tip #9

Look for Free Baby Boxes

Some companies like to say 'congratulations' just for having a baby. They congratulate you by sending you a few baby freebies! Now, not every company advertising to send out 'freebie boxes' is legitimate. Be careful if you are requesting a free baby box that you are making this request from a reliable company. Be sure you are not getting scammed.

Here are a few companies from which I requested freebies when I was pregnant:

Amazon.com

Amazon has a feature that allows Prime members to use the program Jumpstart to create a baby registry. If you create a complete baby registry, and have over $10 in orders from your Amazon baby registry, then you receive a free baby registry welcome box.

Although I didn't need many things for our second baby, I created a baby registry with Amazon anyway, so that I could take advantage of this deal. I included a couple of things on the registry that I actually needed. I then ordered those items, and thus was eligible to receive a free baby box. The box I received from Amazon contained a number of items – some items for baby and some for me.

Sam's Club

My husband and I are members of Sam's Club. If you already have a Sam's Club membership, there is no purchase obligation to receive these baby freebies. Just fill out a request for a free baby sample box, and Sam's Club will send a box of goodies to your doorstep!

Target and Buy Buy Baby

Both Target and Buy Buy Baby reward you with goodie bags when you sign up for baby registries with their companies! These goodie bags are typically full of great samples. The goodie bag I received from Buy Buy Baby included items such as a few diapers, a small package of wipes, samples of lotions/rash creams/etc., an Avent bottle, baby food samples, and tons of coupons! Simply set up a registry in-store with either of these companies to receive a bag of baby freebies!

As a side note...I am sure there are other stores with similar offers. So, if you don't have a Target or Buy Buy Baby in your area, check out your local stores to see who might offer a goodie bag with the creation of a baby registry.

Similac, Enfamil, and Gerber

As mentioned during Tip #3 regarding breastfeeding and formula feeding, be sure to request samples from formula companies. These are great freebies to receive and they typically come complete with coupons! I received samples and/or coupons from Similac, Enfamil, and Gerber.

I have provided you with a number of suggestions for free baby boxes, so if you are expecting be sure to request as many freebies as possible. I know that there are other companies that offer free baby items. There are lots of mom blogs that outline the best freebies to grab before baby arrives, so read up. Don't be afraid to request these freebies, just be sure they are from trusted companies.

chapter three
Food: The Budget Buster

We have pretty well covered my best tips for cutting costs while raising a baby and a toddler. Let's move on to another high-ticket area of most people's budgets...food.

When we talk with people, we find that the food budget is one of the categories that most often frustrates people. Some people report struggling to make choices at the grocery store and leave with unnecessary items in their cart. While other people are trying to feed a big family of hungry teenagers and feel like their grocery budget is out of control. Grocery budgets look very different for each family. It various depending on the size of family, the location where you live (different locations will contribute to very different prices for food products), and the time you are able to dedicate to food preparation. However, whatever the size of your budget or your situation, we have tips that are applicable to everyone!

And let's face it, no matter how crazy you get with cutting costs in your budget as you are paying off debt (or whatever your financial goal), you still need to be able to feed your family. Food is a must.

And if you are like me, you want your family to be able to eat the healthiest, most well rounded diet possible on a minimal budget. In this next section, I will share what I've learned these last couple of years as a 'domestic engineer' in regards to feeding my family.

My husband found that a few of his hobbies also came in handy in regards to making food more affordable. If you enjoy hunting and fishing or have friends that do, it might be time to expand your palate. Our debt-free journey introduced me foods that I would have never tried otherwise. Meats like venison, goose, pheasant, as well as a variety of fish started popping up in our diet. Although I still prefer chicken and beef, I have become accustomed to some of these other meat varieties, and I am not quite as scared when my husband cooks dinner.

Tip #10
Never Buy Full-Priced Meat

Protein is an important part of my family's diet. But, when my husband and I got married and I first started cooking for the two of us – planning the meals and buying the groceries – I quickly realized that meat was the *most* expensive category in my grocery budget. I felt that cutting back on our consumption of meat was not an option (we don't eat a large amount of meat as we include other protein sources in our diet), so I knew I needed to find a way to cut the costs of meat in my grocery budget.

This is a cost cutting method that took me quite a while to figure out, but with time I found a routine that works quite well for our family. So, what is my tip? Simply put, I never (never ever) buy full-priced meat. I'm going to share some specific ways to avoid full-priced meat, so here are some of my best tips:

Watch for rotating sales.

Every grocery store rotates their sale items. As long as there isn't a disease outbreak that kills off a bunch of chickens (that happened during our first year of marriage and the price of chicken and eggs skyrocketed), you can pretty much guarantee that chicken breasts will go on sale at least once a month…once every two months at the very least.

So, I wait until a specific type of meat goes on sale, and then I stock up! Meaning, if this week chicken breasts are selling for just $2.00 per pound or less, you can be sure that I am going to buy about ten pounds of chicken. That's a great price for chicken (in our area), and ten pounds of chicken will last us at least two months. That's plenty of time to make sure that chicken breasts will be on sale again before I run out. Or, for example, if ground beef is on sale for $1.68 per pound, I am going to be stocking up because I know that is the cheapest ground beef price I will find at our local grocery stores or Wal-Mart.

Buy in bulk.

I have learned that many times, you will find your best priced meat in three pound packages or greater. Once again, you are rewarded for buying in bulk! I have been known, on more than one occasion, to come home with a ten-pound chub of ground sausage. Yes, ten pounds! My husband was more than impressed when I walked thru the door toting that quantity of meat!

If you are looking to save money on meat, you could also consider buying a whole cow. In our area, it is common for local butcher shops to sell a fourth, a half, or an entire cow. If you have enough freezer space, you can buy a cow or a portion of a cow. You could also go in on a purchase like this with a friend or another family member. This is a large purchase upfront, but when you consider cost per pound, once again this 'buying in bulk' option is definitely cost-effective!

We often buy in bulk when a certain type of meat goes on sale. We are able to buy in bulk, in part, due to the fact that we have a deep freezer. I am serious when I say that a deep freezer was one of the best investments we ever made! Deep freezers are really not expensive (in comparison to most appliances). You can get a small deep freeze for about $200. I know for certain that our deep freezer has saved us way more than $200. It has allowed us to stock up on much cheaper meat, store large quantities of breast milk (so we avoided the expense of formula), and it's held quite a bit of hunted game meat, which has also saved us money as my husband butchers and processes his own meat. That being said, if you are considering buying in bulk, a deep freezer might be a worthwhile purchase for your household.

Purchase reduced-price meat.
Another money saving option when buying meat is to look for reduced-price meat. In our area, Wal-Mart and both of our local grocery stores offer reduced-price meat. Reduced-price meat is typically meat that is about to exceed its 'best if used by' date. The catch is that this meat only goes bad if it is not used or frozen before that date. I often save money by buying this reduced-price meat and sticking it in the freezer to use later. Just recently I purchased about three pounds of pork chops for $5.66!

Meal plan based on meat sales.
Plan your meals in accordance with the meat sales. Don't plan a meal that will require you to purchase meat that isn't on sale. Rather, always stock up when prices are low. That way you will have a selection of low-cost meat in your freezer to choose from for cooking!

Cook with less meat.
My last 'meat tip' pertains to the amount of meat that you use. Be careful not to use more meat than necessary for a recipe. The 'necessary' amount will vary based on the size of your family.

For example, I cook for a family of four, two of whom are toddlers and don't eat nearly as much as teenagers. For our family of four, I *never* use more than one pound of ground hamburger when I am making a meal, and even one pound will leave us with a few leftovers. I am likely to bulk up a dish with additional rice, beans, or vegetables (which are cheaper options) rather than cooking more meat. For example, when I cook meat for tacos, I add two cans of black beans. The beans add great protein and make the meat go farther, guaranteeing enough leftovers for at least one more meal. The only time that I use more than one pound of meat in a dish is if I am cooking in bulk and am going to put some of the food in the freezer.

Serve at least one meat-free dinner each week.
When we think of serving a meal, we often picture a nicely set table with a main course meat, multiple sides including vegetables, potatoes, and buns, and a sweet dessert to finish. I'm here to say…a picture perfect dinner is *not* necessary to feed your family. Simply eliminating meat from your meal can significantly reduce your dinner costs. In fact, some of our family's favorite dinners are meatless including egg bake with hashbrowns, pancakes or waffles with a side of eggs, vegetable stir fry, and knoephla soup, to name a few. You can even substitute beans for meat in many meals that commonly include meat. This can be done with tacos, spaghetti, and hamburgers (I guess 'bean burgers' in this case), to name a few.

There are a number of different and effective ways to lower the cost of meat in your grocery budget. However, be patient with yourself as you incorporate this tip. It will take you time to learn the sales at your local grocery stores and to figure out the best prices in your area for different kinds of meat. But, once you really get in the groove with this tip, I know your grocery budget will be much more manageable!

Tip #11
Cook – Don't Buy Pre-Made

Have you ever noticed that frozen, pre-made meals typically cost quite a bit more than the ingredients to make those meals? In our area, a good-quality frozen dinner costs on average about $4.00. I say 'on average' because you can find cheaper frozen dinners for around $2.50, while other healthier frozen dinners are between $5.00 and $6.00. Some of the gluten free frozen dinners that would work for my special diet cost even more.

If I considered buying a frozen dinner for both my husband ($4.00) and me ($6.00), plus a kids frozen dinner for each of our girls ($2.00 per meal), I would spend about $14.00 for one meal! Now, let's suggest for a moment that I was to buy a family-size frozen dinner for my whole family to eat, such as lasagna. I can get a family-size frozen lasagna for about $12.00, but that doesn't include any sides such as vegetables or garlic toast.

On the contrary, let's take a look at a typical meal cooked for our family – a dinner of homemade chili and cornbread with a side of green beans. To make homemade chili, I use the following ingredients:

~ 1 pound of hamburger – no more than $2.00
~ 4 cans of beans – $0.68 each for a total of $2.72
~ 2 cans of diced tomatoes – from our pantry of homegrown and home canned food…$0.00
~ 2 cans of tomato sauce – also from our pantry…$0.00
~ Chili powder and few other seasonings – very minimal cost

Then, for the cornbread, we need a few ingredients from our

pantry (again, it is a minimal cost for a bit of cornmeal, gluten free flour, baking soda, etc.) and a cup of sour cream (less than $1.00). The green beans, also found in our pantry, would cost $0.00.

In total, this dinner would cost around $6.00. That is less than half of what I would spend to feed my family on frozen dinners. And a pot of chili that size along with a pan of cornbread will feed my family for about three meals, so that's actually only $2.67 per meal!

Even if I needed to purchase the items that were in our pantry, this whole meal would still only cost approximately $10.00-$12.00, breaking down to about $3.33-$4.00 per meal. Now, there are times that cooking a meal for my family may cost a bit more than this. Regardless, cooking is still much cheaper than buying frozen dinners!

Compare $2.67 to $14.00, and there is no reason every family shouldn't be cooking! It does take more time to cook your own meals, but it is a *huge* cost saver in the long run, and you get to choose what your family is eating!

Make It Yourself

There are many staples we use in the kitchen that can be purchased in the store, but are cheaper to make at home.

One example of this is spice mixes – taco seasoning, chili seasoning, and ranch seasoning to name a few. You will notice, in my previous example of homemade chili, I use my own combination of chili powder and other seasonings instead of buying a packet of chili seasoning. Why? It's *way* cheaper to use my own spices and I get to decide how spicy to make my chili. I can really personalize it!

Another item found in many recipes is cream soups – cream of chicken soup, cream of mushroom soup, etc. It's so easy to buy a can of cream soup at the store and dump it in your casserole. However, with a little bit of butter, milk, broth, flour, and a few seasonings, you can easily and more cheaply make any variety of cream soup at home. Because I am gluten free, this tip is an even bigger cost saver for my family. One can of gluten free cream of mushroom soup costs anywhere from about $1.50 to $3.00. I can make my own for less than $0.50. Some meals I create for my family take two cans of cream soup. That's a savings of upwards of $5.00 by making it myself!

Freezer Meals

I know that one of the biggest reasons people opt to buy frozen dinners is a lack of time to cook. Pre-made, frozen dinners are faster and more convenient. If you are someone who needs a faster, more convenient option, I would encourage you to make your own freezer meals. I have made many freezer meals. Let's face it, I have two small children and I also need quick, easy dinner options at times.

How do you get started? Pinterest and mom blogs are full of freezer meal collections. Many times, these freezer meal postings come complete with all of the recipes, a shopping list, and the approximate cost to create. All of the prep work is done for you. You just have to go shopping and cook! If you dedicate a few hours one day, you can easily prep a dozen or more freezer meals and have some quick dinner options for weeks to come!

Meal Planning

When you are thinking about cooking for you and your family, it's important that you stay organized and have a plan. You don't want to be running to the grocery store every day because that gets expensive. Meal planning is the answer to this organization! If you're wondering, *"What in the world is meal planning?"* then look below at an example of my meal planning.

Sunday – Stir Fry (chicken and vegetables), Rice, Watermelon
Monday – Zuppa Toscana Soup, Spinach Salad, GF Buns, Fruit
Tuesday – Leftovers

Wednesday – Creamy Chicken and Broccoli, Vegetables, Rice, Fruit

Thursday – Waffles, Scrambled Eggs with Peppers and Spinach, Blueberries, Yogurt

Friday – Pizza, Spinach Salad, Applesauce

Saturday – Zucchini Bake, Roasted Beets over Spinach, Fruit

Sunday – Travel Day – Sandwiches, Fruit, and Vegetables on the road

Monday – Knoephla Soup, Vegetables, Applesauce

Tuesday – Tuna Melts, Vegetables, Fruit Salad

Wednesday – Baked Whole Chicken, Potatoes, Vegetables

Thursday – Chicken and Rice Soup (leftover chicken plus vegetables), GF Buns, Fruit

Friday – Spaghetti, Spinach Salad, Applesauce

Saturday – Leftovers

You will notice that I don't plan a whole month at a time. That's way too much for me to wrap my brain around! Instead, I plan two weeks at a time. If you want to do a whole month, go for it! But, you can just use part of your allotted grocery budget and plan half a month at a time!

I also plan only evening meals in my meal planning. Here's why...

Breakfast

Breakfast in our house is simple. Choices include toast, cereal, oatmeal, eggs, muffins, pancakes, yogurt/fruit, or some combination of that. Most of those things are either pantry items that I stock up on during sales (cereal, pancake/muffin ingredients, and oatmeal) or items that I buy on a weekly/bi-weekly basis (eggs, bread for toast, and yogurt).

Lunch

Lunch is leftovers from dinner, sandwiches, salads, fruit, a pile of vegetables…basically anything easy and healthy! I don't see a point a "cooking" two meals a day.

So, I meal plan dinners and that is it. I still obviously include breakfast and other food items in my grocery budget (when I make a grocery list of the things I need to buy, I include those items on there), but I don't plan out what we will eat each morning!

Also, you will notice that I often write just "vegetables" or "fruit." I leave this open ended because I don't always know what produce will be on sale or what I will get in my order from Bountiful Baskets. I plan the main portion of our meal, and then I get creative with fruits and vegetables based on what's in my fridge!

If you're new to the idea of meal planning and want more help, once again mom blogs and Pinterest are full of great meal planning tips! In addition, there are some apps dedicated solely to meal planning. On these apps, you can find and store recipes, and have the app generate your shopping list according to your selected recipes.

'Easy or Cheap Meals'

When you're cooking remind yourself, like I mentioned previously, that you don't have to serve up a picture perfect meal every night. Growing up, I remember that about once a week, we would have an 'easy meal' or a 'cheap meal' – whatever you want to call it. An easy meal meant we might be eating a bowl of oatmeal or cold cereal with a piece of toast, or maybe tuna melts (tuna, cheese, and mayo spread over a slice of bread and melted in the microwave). Not only were our 'easy meals' always cheap, but they also gave my mom a night off from cooking.

I have given you quite a few things to consider when it comes to cooking at home. No matter how many of my tips you employ, I guarantee that doing more of your cooking at home rather than eating out or buying pre-made meals will always be a cost cutter.

Tip #12
Freeze or Can Produce

Have you ever noticed that produce is so much cheaper when it is actually in season? In order to save money on produce, our family buys produce in bulk during the summer when it is in season. (Note: We live in North Dakota. If you live somewhere warm with year-round growing seasons, I guarantee that your produce prices and availability will differ greatly from ours!) We then home can or freeze the produce so that we have produce during the fall, winter, and spring. This is actually quite a cost cutter!

To put this into numbers...I buy strawberries, blueberries, and cherries every summer and freeze them. I usually find the best prices and highest quality produce at Sam's Club. During the summer, I can usually buy a one-pound carton of strawberries for about $1.50. During the winter months, one of these one-pound cartons usually costs at least $2.98-$3.98, which is at least two times the summer season cost.

Now, you are probably wondering, why don't you just buy frozen produce at the store? Again, it's much more expensive than buying and freezing my own produce during the summer season. And freezing your own produce is so easy. I just sort through my produce and pick out any bad berries, wash the berries, allow the berries to dry on a towel, and then freeze the berries in two cup portions in Ziploc freezer bags. I do this with blueberries, strawberries, and cherries (although, when I prepare cherries, I add pitting the cherries to the process).

I briefly mentioned that we also home can produce during the summer months. For our family, our fruit canning includes pears, peaches, sometimes cherries, and all things apple (applesauce, apple pie filling, etc.). In addition to canning pears and peaches in a very light simple sugar syrup (much lighter than what you would purchase from the store), I also can pears and peaches in 100 percent fruit juice. I then use these pears and peaches to make pureed baby food, thus cutting costs in the baby food category as well. We also can a variety of vegetables including green beans, carrots, and tomatoes. However, we do not purchase these produce items, but rather grow them in our garden, which I will highlight more in the next tip.

Now, if you don't feel comfortable canning or don't have the supplies to do so, freezing is a perfectly fine option as well! I have frozen sliced peaches, sliced apples, apple pie filling, and applesauce, and have been pleased with my results. Just make sure to treat produce prior to freezing so that it doesn't brown. A quick Google search will give you all the facts you need to know in order to successfully freeze your produce.

Whatever method you prefer – canning or freezing – if you have a fruit-loving family, be sure to buy your produce in bulk when it is in season! By stocking up during the summer months, we avoid buying high-priced produce during the winter and I never buy canned or frozen fruit from the store! It takes some extra work, but in the long run, this is a huge cost saving method for our family!

Tip #13
Plant a Garden

During the summer months, we enjoy planting and tending a garden. Not only is it a fun project for my husband and me (and the kids too), but it saves us money on groceries as well!

Each summer, we fill our garden with our family's favorite produce – produce that we would need to buy at the grocery store if we did not grow it. If you are going to grow a garden of your own, be sure to choose produce that your family will eat!

We choose vegetables such as green beans, peas, carrots, beets, tomatoes, spinach, peppers, potatoes, and onions. During the summer months, the spinach, tomatoes, and peas for our salads come from the garden. We have to purchase spinach during the winter months. But in the summer when we can grow spinach for the minimal price of the seeds (typically just a couple of dollars), we find it absurd to *pay* for spinach.

Many of the vegetables from our garden are home canned or frozen, and saved for the winter months. When we home can our vegetables, we only pay for new canning lids and a little canning salt – both minimal costs. We home can carrots and green beans, so we usually have enough to provide vegetable sides and baby food (made by pureeing the canned vegetables after cooking) for the entire winter. We use our tomatoes to home can a variety of tomato products including diced tomatoes, tomato sauce, and salsa. This may sound crazy, but I almost never shop the canned vegetable section of our grocery store thanks to all of the produce from our garden.

Again, if you are not feeling up to the task of canning, freezing is also a fine option to keep your produce. Just be sure that you have enough freezer space, and don't forget to blanch your vegetables prior to freezing! I have frozen lots of vegetables including diced carrots, chopped onions, and whole cobs of corn.

Avoid Wasting Produce

Food waste is a huge issue, and it isn't limited to the food you grow in your own garden. According to Harvard Law School's Food Law and Policy Clinic and the Natural Resources Defense Council, "Americans throw away $165 billion in wasted food every year." How does this stack up? Well, that means, "As much as 40% of food goes uneaten in the U.S."[1] This issue is not isolated to the U.S. In fact, worldwide one-third of the world's food is lost or wasted every year. When food goes bad and has to be trashed, you are literally throwing away your money. Food waste is a financial and environmental issue; and it's something our family tries our hardest to avoid.

I am speaking from experience when I tell you this…be sure to do your research on how best to keep your vegetables during the winter months. Our first year growing potatoes, I washed all of the potatoes prior to storing them for the winter. That is a big mistake! You are not supposed to wash your potatoes, as that can cause them to not keep as long and even rot. Luckily, we were able to use our potatoes before that happened! But, had we not been so lucky, we would have ended up with wasted produce, which is not at all cost effective.

One last tip to help you avoid wasting produce…every year, in our garden, we plant lots of onions. We use onions in most things that we cook so growing our own onions really cuts down on grocery store costs. Sometimes, however, we struggle to keep our onions from starting to rot. If we notice our onions starting to turn bad, we just dice them up, separate them into one cup portions, and freeze them. They freeze so well and it makes them easy to use! You just grab a bag from the freezer to throw into a meal, and you don't have to worry about dicing.

Look for Free Seeds

Let's face it, seeds don't cost a lot. And, compared to the price of produce you can buy in store, the cost is quite minimal. And, there are even opportunities to get free seeds.

Where can you look for free seeds? Sometimes stores give away old seeds. At the beginning of one summer, a store in our area gave away the remaining seeds from the previous year. We were able to get tons of seeds completely free! In addition, some communities have a seed library. Seed libraries exist to get people excited about growing their own food and provide free seeds to people. In addition to free seeds, some seed libraries offer free educational resources regarding growing your own food.

So, go get your hands a little dirty because with the low cost of seeds and water to grow your garden, you could be saving lots of money on your favorite produce.

Tip #14

Be Careful – Tips on Shopping Sales and Coupons

As Dave Ramsey would say, "Buyer beware!" Believe it or not, shopping the 'sale' or buying the coupon item(s) is not always the cheapest option. You are probably wondering...have I gone crazy? How could I be advocating for *not* choosing a sale price or coupon item? Because, quite frankly, sale prices and coupon items are not always the best deal. Sometimes, as the buyer, you are spending more by taking advantage of the latest sales or coupon items.

Why would I say that coupon items are not always the best deal? Let me explain...

Compare brands and prices.

First of all, many times coupons are for name brand items. Unless you are able to stack coupons, the reduced coupon price on these name brand items still often comes at a higher price than generic items. When you are buying a product, always examine all of the options – coupon items, sales items, and generic items. Search your grocery store shelf from top to bottom. Sometimes the best deal is hidden on a lower shelf, while the brand name coupon item is shelved at eye level. Look at all the available products and compare the cost per unit prices to know which option is the most cost-effective.

Side note: If you are feeling a bit overwhelmed about calculating cost per unit prices and don't want to tote your calculator through the store with you, I have good news for you! If you look on the price tags at your store, chances are good that the cost per unit is listed! At our local stores, next to the total price, the price tag lists the cost per unit (whether that is per pound, per ounce, or per item).

Don't buy items that will expire before you use them.

Secondly, just because the coupon says you can get six bottles of mustard for just $1.00 per bottle, that doesn't mean you should *actually* buy six bottles of mustard! Sometimes people get so caught up in the excitement of 'saving money' they don't consider that they won't use six bottles of mustard before they expire. Only buy what you actually need! If the item is going to expire before you or your family can use it, it is a waste of money.

Don't buy things you don't need.

Finally, just because a coupon is available for a certain product doesn't mean you actually need it! There are many times that our local grocery store offers great coupons for food items that my family doesn't eat and household products that we don't use. If we don't eat or use an item, I don't buy it! Again, only buy what you actually need.

On the flip side, there are many times that using a coupon or shopping the sale is a great idea. For example…

Cost Effective

If the coupon item or sale price is the most cost-effective option for that specific product and you are going to eat or use the product, then absolutely buy it!

If you are looking for even more cost-effective purchases, try 'stacking' your coupon offers. Some stores will allow you to use both a manufacturer coupon and a store coupon on an item. Even if a store doesn't allow coupon stacking in their store policy, you can still use one coupon in-store and submit for cash back on a rebate app or coupon app afterwards. This obviously only works if the printed coupon and the offer on the coupon/rebate app match.

Free Items

Every week, our local grocery store offers a free item. You have to spend $30 or more to receive the free item. But, if I am already planning on spending $30, you can absolutely bet that I am going to take the free item! Even if it is a product my family doesn't often use, I will still take it. It may be a splurge that my family can enjoy, or if it is something we really don't need or use, we can donate it to our local food pantry.

Total Purchase Coupons

I like coupons that are not specific to a certain product, but rather offer a certain amount off of your total purchase. Every once in awhile, our local grocery store offers coupons for $5 off a purchase of $50 or more. Because my husband and I budget on a bi-weekly basis, when a coupon like this is being offered, I will do the bulk of my grocery shopping for the two-week period on that week so that I can receive the coupon discount. Why not receive a $5 discount if I am already planning on spending more than $50 on groceries?

Be sure to shop sales and coupon items when they make sense. But be aware. Always check if the sale or coupon price is actually the lowest price available and never buy unnecessary products just because they are discounted.

Before moving on from this topic of sale prices and making sure you are getting the best price, I want to share one last tip. Make sure to watch the price when you get to the register. Prices are constantly changing, and you want to ensure that you are receiving the price that was listed on the shelf. If one of your items rings up at an incorrect price, request a price check and have the item fixed to reflect the correct price.

Whether you're shopping with a fistful of coupons or not, you have to be aware of all the items on the shelf and know your prices! Don't get caught by bad sales and always make sure to advocate for yourself if you think that something is incorrect.

Tip #15

Pick Your Neighbor's Apples

I am not advising that you dress in black, sneak into your neighbor's backyard in the middle of the night, and pick all of his or her apples to save money. Your integrity is worth a bit more than that! What I am encouraging you to do is to keep your eyes and ears open to neighbors and friends who might have unwanted or extra produce to offer.

For example, my family loves everything rhubarb! We make rhubarb jam, rhubarb juice, rhubarb pie, freeze rhubarb for crisp, and my husband has even been known to make pickled rhubarb. But, when we moved into our home, there was no rhubarb plant in the backyard. (That is actually weird. Most homes in our area have at least one rhubarb plant in the backyard. It is practically a weed around here!) While we immediately planted a rhubarb plant, we knew we couldn't expect a good crop for the first couple of years. So, we asked around. Sure enough! The last two years we have had a number of people volunteer their rhubarb plants for picking.

The same goes for apples. We received two different offers from people to give us apples last year. We canned applesauce and apple pie filling, and froze some sliced apples. This means I haven't purchased any applesauce or pureed apple baby food from the store. In addition, the apple pie filling gave us some low-cost dessert options.

Thanks to friends, family, and random community trees, we have also picked free apricots, crab apples, sweet corn, and pumpkins. So, ask around. Seek out local produce grown in your area. You never know what treats your neighbors may have growing in their backyards!

Tip #16
Let's Talk Coffee

When it comes to the topic of coffee, I've got a few tips for all you 'coffee-loving people.' Although I am not a huge 'coffee person' myself, my husband would be classified as a 'coffee-lover' so this is still a topic I know well.

Avoid buying coffee from a coffee shop.
It's routine for so many coffee-lovers. Every morning on the way to work, you stop by your local coffee shop – Starbucks, Caribou Coffee, you name it. One coffee or other beverage and you have easily spent about $5...on *one* beverage! Assuming you only drink one of these specialty beverages every day, at $5 per day, that is a total of $150 per month. Think about what a dent that would make in your debt if you could apply an extra $150 to your debt payments each month! Or, if you are debt free, think about all of the other things you could do with an extra $150 every month.

   Instead, buy coffee beans or coffee grounds from the store and make your own coffee at home. Or wait until you get to the office, and get the pot going there. Your company pays for that coffee, so why not take advantage of it!

Use a refillable Keurig cup.
Our family has a Keurig and we love, love, love it! Although I am not a coffee-lover, I do like hot cocoa and tea, so we make plenty of beverages with our Keurig. What we don't love is that K-cups are expensive and add unnecessary waste to our landfills. So, we have found other ways to enjoy our favorite

beverages.

For coffee, we have a refillable Keurig cup. Each morning, my husband, scoops some Folgers (or whatever large container of coffee is currently in our cupboard) into the refillable cup and makes his morning cup of coffee. When he is done, the coffee grounds are dumped into a jar to be saved (we put the grounds on our garden…coffee is a great fertilizer), the Keurig cup gets washed, and it is all repeated the next morning.

If I am making hot cocoa, I am going to buy a big container of hot cocoa mix from the store. Again, this is much cheaper than buying the little hot cocoa K-cups that you can use in your Keurig. I simply run the Keurig to make hot water (with nothing in the K-cup compartment), and then add hot cocoa mix or a tea bag to my cup of hot water.

If you are a coffee-lover, take a look at your routine. That daily cup of Starbucks could be keeping you from achieving your financial dreams!

Tip #17

Your Local Fruit Truck, Farmer's Market, or Bountiful Basket Program

If you are a lover of produce, like myself, you probably hate the high prices you find on tags in your local grocery store's produce section. Well, let me tell you about one of our favorite low-cost produce options!

Have you ever heard of the program called Bountiful Baskets? Bountiful Baskets is a food co-op program that distributes produce baskets, organic produce baskets, bread baskets, and baskets with other food items including granola or specific produce items in bulk. These food items are distributed on a weekly or bi-weekly basis, depending on the distribution site.

When we contribute (this is the 'politically correct' term as it is a food co-op), or order, a Bountiful Basket we pay right around $20. This price varies by state, and will be greater if you choose to order an organic basket or select any add-ons. The amount of produce – both fruits and vegetables – that we receive for just $20 is incredible! The price per produce item is much lower than the prices in our grocery stores! In fact, I did the math for one of the baskets that we received and it would have cost me at least $40 to purchase all of that produce at the grocery store.

With Bountiful Baskets, you do not know what you will receive in your basket (add-ons provide more specifications, but the regular baskets do not). However, we have enjoyed the surprise and never have trouble using the produce we receive. It is fun because sometimes we get a fruit or vegetable that we had never even seen before (like baby bok choy); and we have to figure out what to do with it! It has been fun to try some new and different produce items! I have to say...when we order from Bountiful Baskets, the produce part of our diet is much more varied. Feel free to check out the Bountiful Baskets website (www.bountifulbaskets.org) for more information and to find out whether or not this co-op is offered in your area.

If you do not have Bountiful Baskets in your area, I encourage you to look for other food co-ops or clubs, or a local farmer's market. There are many different co-ops and clubs that sell various food items (from produce and meat to nuts and grains) in bulk. There have been a couple of co-ops and clubs that I have looked into where the food items are actually more expensive than the price I find in the grocery store, but generally it is cheaper to purchase food items from a co-op. So, do a little research and see if you can find a co-op in your area that offers food items at a lower price. Your grocery budget will thank you!

Tip #18
Reuse Food Containers

If you are watching your budget and being resourceful with your choices, chances are you are also saving your leftovers...because throwing them would be a huge waste! Well, in order to save those leftovers, you will need some containers to keep your food in the fridge.

Rather than buying expensive Tupperware, we save and reuse the containers from our yogurt, sour cream, and other food products we purchase from the grocery store. Side note: I am not at all opposed to Tupperware. Now that we are debt free, we have actually splurged and purchased some expensive Tupperware. I really like my Tupperware and I think it's worth the extra expense because it is much better quality and comes with a lifetime warranty. But, in the middle of our debt-free journey, buying Tupperware was simply not in the budget!

There are a number of great ways that you can repurpose your old food containers. For example, the first year that we had a garden, we used old yogurt containers and trimmed down milk cartons to start all of our seeds. We had a whole collection of tomato and cucumber plants growing out of these repurposed containers!

You can reuse food containers for organizing small parts such as nails, screws, and drill bits, or small crafts items such as beads or crayons. Empty parmesan cheese containers are perfect for organizing small parts. My dad loves using these to organize the nails and screws he uses for his woodworking projects.

And if you have a toddler, containers can be a source of great fun! My toddler loves just sitting and matching containers and lids. In addition, a collection of small objects and a container can keep a toddler occupied for quite some time as they explore putting objects in and taking them out.

There are countless ways to reuse your food containers. I have offered a few suggestions here, but I guarantee that Google and Pinterest have hundreds of more suggestions just waiting for you.

Tip #19
Rebate and Coupon Apps

Would you like to receive rebates on your grocery and household items? There are a number of apps that offer rebates at various stores. I have tried quite a few of these apps, and my favorite rebate apps are Ibotta and Ebates. This is just my personal preference. You may find that you prefer a different rebate app depending on the stores available in your area or depending on your family's lifestyle needs. A few other rebate apps include: Checkout 51, RetailMeNot, and SavingStar.

Ibotta App

I have been using Ibotta for over a couple years now. I don't use it all of the time, so sometimes it takes me awhile to build up a rebate total on this app, but I do appreciate many of Ibotta's offers.

You do need to be careful when using a rebate app. If you are not cautious, it is easy to find yourself buying unnecessary items just because they are offering a good rebate for that specific item. If earning a rebate means buying a product that you do not need or will not use, you are wasting your money! However, if you are earning a rebate on a product that you do need to buy and will use, then go ahead! So let's talk more about Ibotta.

Ibotta is an app that offers rebates – both in-store rebates and online/mobile shopping rebates. You can search through the Ibotta app to find rebates by store. Once you find the item on Ibotta, you watch a short (and I mean short) video or answer one question to unlock the specific rebate, saving it to your list of rebates. Then, after shopping, you redeem your rebates by scanning the QR code or barcode on the bottom of your receipt or by taking a picture of your receipt. It takes me just a minute to submit my receipt after a shopping trip. Once your receipt is submitted, it is reviewed by Ibotta and your account is credited with your rebate total.

Your rebate earnings on your Ibotta account can be redeemed in a few different ways. You can opt to receive a gift card from one of the following companies: Best Buy, Amazon.com, Walmart, iTunes, Starbucks, Target, Sam's Club, and the list goes on. You need a total of at least $20 to receive one of these gift cards. You can also opt to have your PayPal or Venmo account credited with your total. In order to choose this option, you also must have a total of $20 in your account. I have my PayPal account linked to my Ibotta account. This makes it quick and easy to transfer my earnings to PayPal, which I can then transfer right into our bank account. Because I use Ibotta to earn cash back on grocery, household, and hygiene product purchases, I transfer those earnings back into the appropriate budget categories.

A few of my favorite Ibotta rebates to take advantage of include the following:

Any Brand Rebates

Ibotta offers Any Brand rebates for a variety of different products including milk, cheese, numerous produce items, bread, crackers, cereal, etc. For example, this means that no matter what brand of milk you buy, as long as it matches the size requirement (i.e. half gallon, gallon, whatever is detailed on the rebate!), you can receive money back on that item. I love these rebates because it allows me to buy the generic brand products and still receive a rebate! Essentially, I save money twice!

Ibotta also offers an Any Item rebate. This means that you can purchase *any item* – yes, any item in the store – and you receive $0.25 cash back. It's not a lot of cash back, but you can earn it on *any* purchase you make. This is easy money back! I try to use this offer every time that I shop, as long as the offer is available.

Natural Food Rebates

I feel that so often coupons are aimed at pre-made food items (such as frozen pizza, pizza rolls, microwave dinners, the list goes on). Because of my food allergies and my family's desire to eat a healthier diet, we rarely buy any of these pre-made food items. Thus, I appreciate that Ibotta offers rebates on some natural food items and produce.

For example, I have a peanut butter powder that I buy at Walmart to use in smoothies and baby food. This peanut butter powder is not cheap (about $10 for a 24-ounce jar), but Ibotta recently offered a $2.00 rebate, which made this product a bit more affordable for my family.

Walmart's Savings Catcher App

It is common knowledge that Walmart guarantees their prices as being the lowest. They take pride in this and it's even in their slogan, "Always Low Prices." Well, Walmart has created a tool that makes it easy to guarantee you are receiving the lowest prices. This tool is called the Savings Catcher.

Located within their Walmart app, the Savings Catcher allows you to submit your receipt by scanning the QR code at the bottom of your receipt after making a purchase at Walmart. The Savings Catcher will then compare the prices on your receipt with the prices at other stores in your area. If it finds a store that is offering a lower price on a certain product, you will be reimbursed the difference!

It takes just seconds to scan your receipt and then the Savings Catcher does all the hard work, so using this app is definitely worthwhile! In addition, your receipts are stored on your account for up to one year, so if you need to return something, you can easily access your saved receipt.

Ebates App

I started using the Ebates app more recently. I love using this app for online purchases and honestly wish I would have discovered it sooner. Ebates is a rebate app with in-store, mobile, and online offers – meaning that you can use it on your desktop computer as well, so you don't have to own a smartphone. However, some offers are only available on the Ebates mobile app. Ebates partners with more than 600 stores, which makes for an awesome selection of stores that offer rebates. Here are a few of my favorite things about the Ebates app:

Cash Back on Purchases

Many stores offer a certain percentage back on your total purchase. Some of these offers are mobile/online shopping offers, while some are in-store offers. I love being able to earn cash back on my total purchase. I recently made an online purchase from The Children's Place and received two percent back on my total purchase. If you choose to redeem an in-store offer, you simply link a card to your Ebates account, save that store's rebate offer to your card, and use that card to make your in-store purchase. After making the purchase, your purchase will be automatically reviewed and your account credited with the appropriate cash back.

Now, be advised that some of these total cash back offers have exclusions – certain products or store categories might not be available for cash back. Be certain to read the fine print before making a purchase where you hope to receive cash back.

Coupon Codes and Sales

In addition to offering rebates, Ebates also lists coupon codes and sales available at each store on both their app and their website. In addition to receiving cash back on your order, you can choose to use those coupon codes or shop those sales when you check out, thereby further lowering the cost of your purchase.

Double and Triple Cash Back Events

Ebates holds special double and triple cash back events where stores, like the event name implies, offer double or triple of their typical cash back offers. Meaning, if JCPenney typically offers three percent back on any purchase, during a Double Cash Back event, they will usually offer at least six percent cash back, sometimes more. These events are often hosted in coordination with a certain holiday – special romantic offers around Valentine's Day, lots of extra offers at Christmas time when everyone is purchasing last-minute gifts, sweet deals on Black Friday, and the list goes on. These are awesome times to make your purchases and earn even more cash back!

Ebates pays on a quarterly basis. According to the official Ebates website, their payment schedule is as follows:

Purchases Posted Between	Big Fat Check Sent
Jan. 1 – March 31	May 15
Apr. 1 – June 30	Aug. 15
July 1 – Sept. 30	Nov. 15
Oct. 1 – Dec. 31	Feb. 15

You can choose to receive your Ebates Big Fat Check in one of two ways. You can enter your home address and Ebates will send you a check in the mail. Or you can link PayPal to your account and have your cash back transferred straight into your PayPal account. I, once again, prefer PayPal as it is faster and more convenient to use. If you would rather give your earnings, you can also opt to send your Big Fat Check to a charity, organization, or family member.

Coupons.com App and/or Website

Coupons.com offers both an app and a website that are awesome to use! The Coupons.com app offers certain coupons by store. They partner with tons of stores, so chances are good that there is a store in your area where you can use the Coupons.com app. Here's how you use the app:

- ~ Browse the coupon offers available at the store you wish to shop.
- ~ Select the coupons that you want to use on your shopping trip.
- ~ Go to the store and purchase these items.
- ~ After making your purchases, take a picture of your receipt and submit the receipt for review.
- ~ Once your receipt has been reviewed, you receive cash back in the amount of your selected coupons. It usually only takes a couple of days for a receipt to be reviewed. I had one receipt take a week to be reviewed when submission volumes were high.
- ~ You can then have this cash automatically transferred to your PayPal account and, without much work on your part, you have been paid!

I love using the Coupons.com app. It is user-friendly, and I don't have to fret that my coupon might not scan. Plus, the app makes submitting receipts a breeze and I don't have to pay for printer ink and paper to print coupons. I know ink and paper don't cost *that* much, but I like to cut down on our printing costs where we can…and save a few trees along the way.

You can also choose to use the Coupons.com website. Although I often use the app, there are a couple of reasons I sometimes print coupons from their website. Firstly, there are times that they have offers available from their printable coupons that are not available on the app. Secondly, if you print a coupon and use it in the store, it is taken off pre-tax. Check out this graph detailing the cost benefits of using a printed coupon. The example here is based on using a $3.00 off coupon to purchase BIC Soleil razors (3 count), which typically retail for $3.27 plus tax.

Coupon Method	Product	Price	Tax*	Paid in Store	Cash Back	Total
App	BIC razors	$3.27	$0.20	$3.47	$3.00	$0.47
Printed Coupon	BIC razors	$0.27**	$0.02	$0.29	$0.00	$0.29

*Tax is calculated based on a 7% sales tax.
**$3.27 (retail price) minus $3.00 (coupon) equals $0.27.

You can see that for this particular example, there is only a difference of $0.18 in using the app versus using a printed coupon. This may seem like a minuscule difference. However, let's say you go to the store and use coupons totaling $10 off your purchase. Now, you have saved $0.60 in tax. My general principle…if it is a coupon for a higher dollar amount, I am most likely going to print it as the tax savings are worth the cost printing the coupon. Side note: You can actually print their printable coupons from the app on your smartphone or from the Coupons.com website on your computer. You are limited to a certain number of printed coupons per device. Meaning, if you reach your printing limit for a specific coupon on your computer, you can pull up that coupon on your phone and print more copies.

My favorite part of using the Coupons.com app is taking advantage of their free items. Many weeks, they offer one or two items that are free up to a certain price point. I have gotten free bananas, eggs, oranges, milk, avocados, bread, and much more! When purchasing a free item, you once again pay upfront and then are reimbursed up to the specific price point listed on the coupon offer. For example, when the Coupons.com app had a coupon for free eggs, they offered reimbursement up to $2.50 on any one package of eggs.

When I use these free item offers, as long as my family will use a large amount of that food item, I typically buy as much as I can for the listed maximum reimbursement. So, I am going to buy the biggest package of eggs that I can for $2.50. Also, remember that if you have a spouse, you can take advantage of these offers twice. I have downloaded each of these apps – Ebates, Ibotta, and Coupons.com – onto my husband's phone and have created accounts for him. I did this with the sole intention of making sure that our family could take advantage of certain coupon and rebate offers more than once. If we are going to use it, why not save on it twice! Just remember, you have to make the purchases on two different receipts because you cannot submit the same receipt twice on two different accounts. This does not mean that you need to take two trips to the store. Instead, just request that your cashier ring up your items in two separate transactions.

Here's a fun story for you from a recent trip to Walmart to purchase my free eggs:

Another side note: Before, I go further with this story, you should know that my husband loves pickling eggs. Well, truthfully he loves pickling most anything, but eggs happen to be one of his favorites. However, since a dozen eggs fit in each quart jar, that hobby can get expensive really fast. So, our agreement is that he pickles eggs when they go on a really good sale.

Back to my story…I had just returned home from my trip

to Walmart. I was unpacking my grocery bags, as my husband was preparing dinner. As I pull out a package of three dozen eggs, I say, "If you don't love me after this..." He glances over, but doesn't really seem intrigued until he sees me pull out yet another package of three dozen eggs. Now, I have perked his interest.

With a big grin and that 'look' in my eyes (my husband says I have a certain look in my eyes – a glimmer that is always present when I have scored a good deal and saved our family money) I say, "Six dozen eggs for $2.00." Now, he is visibly impressed.

So how did I score this awesome deal? Well, our Walmart sells packages of three dozen eggs for just $3.48. I purchased two packages of these eggs, each package purchased on a different transaction. Upon returning home, I submitted one receipt for reimbursement on my Coupons.com account and one on my husband's account. Each of us was reimbursed $2.50 for the eggs, resulting in each package of eggs only costing $0.98. So, to be exact, I actually only spent $1.96 on six dozen eggs. My pickled-egg-loving-husband was able to pickle to his heart's content, and my grocery budget didn't suffer at all!

Be aware of a couple of things when you are using coupons from Coupons.com. If you have a printed coupon and an app coupon for the same product, you cannot stack them. Coupons.com will only allow you to use one coupon offer per product. Meaning, if you have used a paper coupon for a product in the store, you cannot submit that receipt for the same mobile coupon. You can, however, use the paper coupon for one purchase of that product and a mobile coupon for another. This is allowed!

Secondly, be informed of store policies whenever you are using coupons. For example, Wal-Mart is a great place to use coupons from

Coupons.com. However, their policy regarding the input of coupons recently changed. It used to be that if your coupon didn't scan correctly, the cashier could punch it in by hand. This is no longer the case. Now, if your coupon does not scan correctly (this has only happened to me once), you cannot use that coupon. Wal-Mart also only allows one coupon per product, meaning you cannot stack coupons. Additionally, they reserve the right to limit the number of identical coupons used per transaction.

While these rules may seem limiting, Wal-Mart has many positive components to its coupon policy including that they will accept competitors' coupons. You can read the specifics of Wal-Mart's coupon policy on their official website. The policy is a basic, bullet-point list that is very easy to read. I encourage you to familiarize yourself with this policy before using any coupons at Wal-Mart.

Using apps such as those highlighted in this section hasn't saved me thousands by any means. But, when you are on a tight budget and you're trying to get the most bang for your buck, then these apps are sure helpful! I do my best to stock up when good offers present themselves on both the Ibotta app and the Coupons.com app. The table on the following page illustrates a few examples of products that I have purchased using 'stacked' offers. Stacking offers significantly reduced the price of each product. Side note: All of these items were purchased at Walmart.

Product	Retail Price	Coupons/Rebates Used	Final Price
Sport Compact Tampons (18 ct.)	$3.97	Coupons app – $2.00 off*	$1.97
Organic Kids Whole Milk Yogurt	$3.97	Coupons app – $1.00 off Ibotta – $1.00 cash back	$1.97
Caesar Salad Dressing	$2.98	Coupons app – $1.00 off Ibotta – $1.00 cash back	$0.98
Woolite's At-Home Dry Cleaner (6 ct.)	$8.88	Coupon – $2.00 off** Ibotta – $3.00 cash back	$3.88

*This offer was also available as a printed coupon, so I took advantage of using the printed coupon on another shopping trip.
**I found this coupon on Woolite's website. It is always a good idea to check product websites for manufacturer coupons!

While I didn't get any of these products for free, you can see that by stacking coupon and rebate offers, I was able to cut the price at least in half, even by two-thirds with some of these products. I am not expecting a TV show for my coupon savings but you can see how principles like this can be used to save you some serious money! This doesn't have to consume your life. This can be achieved by using a few coupons whenever possible. It doesn't take a ton of time. Once or twice a week, browse the offers on these coupon and rebate apps. Identify any offers you might want to take advantage of and go shopping. Money saved is money towards your goals, and *that* is a great feeling of freedom!

Before moving on to our next topic, I want to share with you a story. It is a story of a conversation that began with a bunch of coupons.

One night, our three-year-old walked up to me with this fistful of coupons and some cash. (She had found my wallet sitting on the nightstand.) She said, "Mommy, we need to take these to Walmart." This made me stop and think.

You see, when we shop at Walmart, I often use the self checkout. I do this because our three-year-old likes to scan our items. It's her favorite part of shopping! Not only is she allowed to scan our items, she also scans our coupons, inserts the cash to pay, and puts the change back in my wallet.

As I thought, I realized that simply by involving our toddler, I was teaching her about finances. I was teaching her about paying for our items. I was teaching her about the exchange of coupons and cash.

Now, at three, she doesn't really understand all of the details of this transaction, but we are setting a foundation.

I have a message for all of you parents…no matter your child's age, involve them in your finances! It is our job to teach our children to be good stewards of God's blessings and what a better way to do that then by allowing them to be a part of it!

chapter four
All Things Insurance

I want you to take a look at your budget over the past year. Pay special attention to the amount that you have paid for insurance – including home or renter insurance, car insurance, health insurance, dental insurance, etc. If you are like our family prior to our debt-free journey, chances are you will find that your insurance is costing you an exorbitant amount.

To give you a perspective…a few years ago, before making some insurance changes, we were paying over $800 *every month* for health care insurance. And this only included coverage for my husband and our first daughter (our second daughter was not yet born, and I was still on my family's insurance plan). But, seriously, $800 for just health insurance *every month* to insure two very healthy people! My husband goes to the doctor less than once a year for a physical; and the only clinic visits our daughter had made at the time we evaluated our health insurance policy were well child checkups. Why should we pay $9,600 per year for two healthy people?

So, you've probably already guessed it…we are going to dedicate the next few pages to talking about how we cut costs with all things insurance. I am relying on my husband to help with the details and the verbiage in this section because, quite frankly, this is not my area of expertise. For our family, when it comes to choosing insurance, my husband shops around. He looks through the coverage offered by different policies, finds the best rates, and then comes to me with his top three choices or so. Then, together we make the decision that we feel is best for our family and our budget.

Tip #20
Consider a High Deductible Insurance or a Health Savings Plan

No matter which party you are voting, I think everyone can agree that the current healthcare system is quite expensive. Here are some tips on how you can lower the cost of your health insurance.

High Deductible Insurance

Like I mentioned before, following the birth of our first daughter, we were paying $800 *every month* in health insurance premiums. We are now paying approximately $237 every month. What changed? Well first of all, we changed our policy from a low deductible policy to a high deductible policy. Our deductible went from $500 to $6,500. That was a *huge* change in deductible and one that made me a little nervous (at first).

Here is how this huge change in our deductible actually worked in our favor. Once we changed our policy, we freed up $563 every month – money that had been previously used to pay for our high deductible plan. Close your eyes and imagine having an extra $563 *every month*. That is groceries, gas, a child's glasses, or a great start to paying off debt by increasing your monthly payments. In our case, we applied the savings to our debt payments. My nerdy husband tells me this fast tracked our debt payments, allowing us to pay off our debt a whole six months prior to our original goal!

But, you're probably wondering…what about the added risk? That is exactly why I was freaked out by a high deductible plan. I thought…what if something happens and we don't have the money for the hospital bill? For that, we relied on our emergency fund of $1,000 and our ability to pull back the amount we were paying on our debt, in the case of a medical emergency.

Now, in actuality, there's an even better way to go about having a high deductible plan and still having a sense of security. Take the savings (that's $563 per month in our example), and put it in a separate savings account earmarked for medical expenses. Rather than sending a big check to the insurance company every month, you keep that extra cash in case of a medical emergency. This new plan puts $6,756 aside each year for medical emergencies – money that was previously being handed to your insurance company. Within one year, you will likely have an account totaling the new deductible of your high deductible policy! Thus, I no longer freak out about our high deductible plan. We have the money set aside; and we have planned in advance for an emergency. What a novel idea!

High deductible plans come in many different forms and some of these plans might not work for you and your family, so be sure to do your research. The premise behind high deductible plans is simple. You pay more before the insurance kicks in, but the premiums (the monthly/yearly payments) are lower. After we reach our deductible of $6,500, the insurance covers 100 percent of our medical expenses.

However, as I mentioned before, these high deductible plans are not for everyone. There is a good reason we opted for me to stay on my family's insurance until I reach the age of 26. These high deductible plans work if you are very healthy, or very sick (i.e. chronic health problems that will result in you meeting your deductible quickly and having the rest of your large expenses covered in full). However, if you are like me (asthma, allergies, and two pregnancies/deliveries within seventeen months resulting in regular chiropractic and physical therapy care), then you might need a different plan.

Health Savings Account
Another great option to save money on medical expenses is by using a Health Savings Account (HSA). An HSA allows you to invest pre-

tax dollars into a special account (known as a Health Savings Account), which is designated for health expenses only. By doing this, you will end up paying less for healthcare because the money you are using to pay your medical bills has not been taxed. Some companies even match your HSA contributions, similar to that of a 401(k) or 403(b), or give you a yearly bonus for having an HSA account.

HSA's can almost be described as an IRA (Individual Retirement Account) on steroids! Not only are HSA contributions tax-deductible, but once you invest the money in the HSA it grows…wait for it…tax free! In addition, when you turn 65, you can use this money for whatever you want without being penalized. If you want to buy a car, go for it! The money is yours.

One short example for you regarding Health Savings Accounts:

Let's say you have a $1,000 medical bill. If this is paid out of an HSA you will have effectively paid your bill by using only $750 because the $1,000 you used to pay was never taxed (that's assuming you are in the 25 percent tax bracket…numbers will vary based on your tax bracket). The government has made loopholes for us to succeed. It is up to us to find them.

Remember, the Health Savings Account rolls over from year to year and follows you even if you change employers or health insurance plans. You also save on taxes in three different ways. First, the money goes into your HSA account pre-tax so your taxable income is less for the year. Second, the money invested in the HSA account grows tax-free. Third, any withdrawal for qualified health expenses from the HSA account is not taxed. So, there is absolutely no reason you shouldn't put this book down right now and open up an HSA account.

In summary, here's my advice when it comes to reducing the cost of your health care insurance and medical expenses. Do some research. Look into different insurance policies – specifically policies with higher deductibles and lower premiums. Seriously consider opening an HSA account...and by 'seriously consider,' I mean 'do it now!' Thoroughly research your options and make a plan that will work best for you and your family. Bottom line...healthcare is expensive and if you can get this sewn up, it could save your family thousands *every single year*!

Tip #21
Re-Evaluate Car and Home Insurance

According to a report by the Insurance Information Institute, 56% of homeowners and 31% of drivers don't comparison shop when their policy is up for renewal. That means those individuals could be missing out on new discounts or opportunities to match their coverage to their current circumstances.[1] Why should you pay more if you could easily switch insurance companies and pay less? Many people see home and auto insurance as a 'one and done' situation – meaning, once you have it then you don't need to worry about it. Wrong! The key with *anything* in your budget is to review it often to make sure it is still working for your family.

Re-evaluate your car insurance. Speak with a car insurance agent and ask if there are discounts. Many times, you might be missing discounts and you won't know it unless you ask. Remember, car insurance companies are businesses. They are making money off of you, so they certainly aren't going to tell you upfront about these discounts. They would prefer that you pay their company more, not less. When we got married and moved into our home, while lining up home insurance, my husband took this opportunity to check into our auto insurance once again. He was actually able to get us a discount because our cars were no longer parked in a college dorm parking lot. That makes complete sense since a parking lot is more dangerous for your car than your personal garage or driveway, right?

Just like I suggested with medical insurance, consider increasing your car insurance deductible. Once you start the process of freeing up your cash flow and having more cash on hand in an emergency fund, there is no need for small deductibles. Rather than paying high monthly/yearly premiums and depending on your insurance, you now have the cash available to pay for those not-so-fun car emergencies.

Many car insurance companies will give you discounts for qualities such as having good grades (for students), holding a public service job, taking defensive driving courses, and being a member of certain organizations like Lifetime Fitness or the American Academy of Pediatrics. Do some research on your insurance website to see what discounts they offer. If you are not already a member, consider joining and being involved in one of these organizations.

Home insurance is a bit different but the basic principles remain the same. I feel like this goes without saying but, your home *needs* to be insured in the event of disaster. There are a few different types of coverage that you should consider when choosing your home insurance. Although most people think that they will have "guaranteed replacement coverage," finding those policies on homes less than $500,000 is fairly tricky. With guaranteed replacement coverage, if your house burns down the insurance company cuts you a check for the cost to rebuild your house. In more recent years, the insurance companies have been slammed with people who have purchased these policies for a $200,000 home, then that same home burns down at a value of $500,000. That's a huge hit for the insurance company!

In order to keep from losing money, the insurance companies have almost transitioned completely to the "extended replacement cost" insurance. This puts more responsibility on the homeowners to stay in check with their insurance as their home appreciates. With this type of coverage, the insurance company agrees to pay for the home that you insured for the initial amount. They will also extend the coverage above the value of your home, usually up to 50 percent, in the case that your home has increased in value. Why is this good? If you obtain insurance coverage and then the value of your home increases slightly, they will still give you a check to replace your home. Why is it bad? If you do not reevaluate your home insurance and the value of your home increases substantially, they might not cover the entire cost.

If your home is worth $200,000 (at the time that you purchase your home insurance), the extended coverage will probably cover up to $300,000. However, if you have not been paying attention to your insurance and the value of your home increases to $450,000 and then burns down, the insurance company will only give you $300,000 and you are out the other $150,000! That is a massive financial hit! This actually happened to friends of ours. They purchased a home. Within the first year of owning their home, they made some nice upgrades which increased its value. However, because the home was not appraised following the renovation and their home insurance policy was not updated, the full value of their home was not covered when they lost it in a house fire. It is important, especially if you are doing home renovations, to make sure to update your home insurance.

What if you don't have a home? If you are renting, you need to make sure to have renter's insurance. Your landlord does not carry this insurance for you and any loss of property you experience is not their responsibility (check your lease agreement if you don't believe me). Renter's insurance is fairly inexpensive and can protect you against disaster in many forms. Living in an apartment complex can bring added risks and having renter's insurance is another step you can take to protect you from financial disaster. You might not be an irresponsible individual, but one irresponsible action from the apartment downstairs and all of your belongings could go up in smoke.

When it comes to home and auto insurance, the key is to always do an annual revisit. Rates are constantly changing so don't just set it and forget it. Shop around each year. Look into bundle packages. See if you qualify for discounts. Negotiate better rates. Most importantly, make sure that your coverage matches the needs of your family!

Tip #22

Choose Term Life Insurance
(Or Why Whole Life Insurance is a Scam)

Let me start this by stating one thing: If there is anyone in your life that would be financially devastated if you died, you *need* life insurance! If you are single with no dependents, you probably don't need a ton of insurance – just enough to settle your debts and pay for your burial. However, as life progresses you might need to reevaluate your life insurance. Income goes up and down, people get married and have kids, and retirement grows. As these things change, you will want to take another look at your policies to make sure you have an adequate amount of life insurance.

What is adequate? You need a life insurance policy that is about 10 to 12 times your annual income. For example, if you make $50,000 a year, you need $500,000. If you are married, have kids, own a home with a mortgage, and have tons of debt, you might even want to consider $1,000,000. This may seem like a lot but if something happens to you, your bill payments will continue. Let your family mourn without worrying about how they are going to pay the next bill. Do this for your family to show them that you love them.

Whatever happens, do *not* fall into the trap of whole life insurance. Before I explain the fundamental differences between whole life insurance and term life insurance, I want to share with you a story:

> One day my husband and I had a visit from a whole life insurance salesman. Now, previous to this visit, we had already purchased the life insurance we each needed and knew the mathematics of whole life insurance versus term

insurance in our situation. So, you're probably really wondering...then, *why in the world* would you have a whole life insurance salesman paying you a visit? Well, my husband works as a paramedic. As a responder, he qualified for a small but free 'death and disablement policy' – a benefit that we wanted to have for my husband. Plus, it was free, so why not? However, in order to get the policy, we had to first visit with the insurance salesman.

Now, this salesman did his best to frighten us from every angle and convince us that the life insurance he was offering was absolutely necessary. He talked about our kids dying, my husband getting injured, my husband dying, and the house burning down and the kids not making it out of the house – basically, all of the things that a mother *really* doesn't want to think about. He gave us his whole spiel, and, honestly, he made his offer sound really convincing. His best insurance plan, in the case of both my death and my husband's death, was going to pay out at a total of $20,000, and all for the low price of *just* $400 each month ("just" being the word choice of the salesman). My husband holds a very stoic demeanor in the face of conflict, but even he raised an eyebrow at those numbers. Yikes! In our budget, that's not *just* $400!

When he finally finished his spiel, he looked at my husband and asked what we thought of his offer. He was quite confident that he had just made us the offer of a lifetime and was going to have an easy sale. After all, we were a young, naive, couple with 2 kids, just starting out. Boy, was he in the wrong house!

Up until this point, I had listened quietly throughout the whole spiel allowing my husband to exchange comments with the salesman. However, unbeknownst to the salesman I was still keeping up with the entire conversation. We work together on our finances, and I understand our insurance policies just as well as my husband. This offer insulted and infuriated me. Rather than answering this question, my husband turned to me with a half smile and asked what I thought. I remember thinking... "We are about to show this guy!" (Kindly, of course.)

In a very tactful way, I informed the salesman that his offer was pathetic, offensive, and exceedingly expensive. At this point we already had 20-year fixed term life insurance policies for my husband and myself, with small riders on both of our children. We had a term life insurance policy for my husband that was ten times his annual gross income and we paid $400 *every year* for the policy, just $33 each month. This whole life insurance salesman was trying to get us to pay that much *every month* for a policy that was worth less than one-third of our annual income! What are our kids supposed to do with that? My husband went through the math and explained why our plan was better. He also encouraged this salesman to continue running the numbers later on so he could see that he was selling products that are awful for the consumer. Insurance agents are paid commission on premium so for them, whole life insurance is a better deal and therefore the ideal sale.

By the time the salesman left, I was actually sick to my stomach. That day, I realized that had I not been so well informed about life insurance options, it would have been easy to believe that we needed everything this salesman was offering, especially after they tried to scare me about me dying and leaving our kids cold and alone. These fear tactics work on many consumers because they do not know their options, and are not well informed on what they are buying. I am so thankful that my husband and I knew otherwise!

Now, let's get down to the fundamental differences. Why is whole life insurance (also called universal life, ordinary life, straight life, etc.) a bad option? Like I mentioned in the story I just told, whole life insurance is roughly ten times as expensive as the same amount of coverage with a term life insurance policy. *Ten times*. But, why is it so much more expensive?

When you buy whole life insurance, you pay for the insurance. By paying for this insurance, you secure a certain predetermined cash value amount payable upon your death (this amount is called the payout, death benefit, or face value). Here is where this insurance can get confusing. Whole life insurance not only has an insurance component; it also has a savings account component. That is why the policy is *so* expensive. The majority of your payment goes into this savings account. Therefore, the longer you have the policy, the more the cash value builds. Some policies invest that value and it grows as investments do, over time. Whole life insurance companies pitch this as the best life insurance option because you can use this cash amount as an emergency fund or invest it as an extra retirement account. Here is the problem. When you die, your beneficiaries will *not* get any of the money you put into this account. They will receive just the predetermined cash value amount. So what happens to the cash value you have paid so much for? Well, apparently they keep it.

There are many people who use a whole life insurance policy to invest money for retirement. However, there is always a better option than whole life insurance. If that was your plan, don't do it. Insurance agents might flaunt charts and graphs that show you making 8 to 12 percent returns on your money, but this is only a half-truth. The full truth is that they fee you into oblivion. According to Consumer Reports, your whole life insurance policy will gain 1.5 percent per year and it can take up to three years to just break even.[2] With inflation, you would be better off burying your money in a bucket in your backyard.

To see the whole life insurance scam in action, look at your statement and find your surrender value. Your surrender value is the value of your money after those fees I mentioned – your 'cash out' value. If you have a whole life policy, you need to put this book down, get a term insurance policy, and then *cancel* your whole life policy. The lesson here is this: I don't want my hair stylist working on my car. I don't want my doctor replacing my gutters. And, I don't want my insurance agent managing my investments!

Might I present you with a better option? Let me offer you term life insurance. This will not take as long to explain because, quite frankly, it's not complicated. With term life insurance, you are simply paying for an insurance policy for a set time frame. In our case, we both have term insurance policies set for 20 years. During those 20 years, the policy does not change, nor does the amount that you pay per year. As mentioned before, when shopping for insurance, you are looking for a policy that is 10 to 12 times your annual income. Why 10 to 12 times? With that amount, if my husband dies, I can take the life insurance money and invest it in good growth-stock mutual funds. Each year, the money will grow and my children and I can live off of just the interest. Essentially, my husband is financially replaced. I cannot fully describe how much security I feel knowing that if something were to happen, we would be financially okay. It is one less thing to worry about. This is one way my husband shows me that he loves me.

Here is an example of a healthy, 30-year old male named John Doe looking for life insurance. John makes $50,000 a year and he wants to get a policy totaling the recommended amount of 10 times his annual salary. With a term life insurance policy, this table shows John investing the monthly difference (the difference between the whole life insurance premium and the term life insurance) in a growth-stock mutual fund averaging 10 percent.

	Whole Life Insurance	30-year Term Life Insurance
Policy	$500,000	$500,000
Premium	$5,376 annual	$390 annual
Difference		$415.50/month
Interest		10%
15 years		$174,259
30 years		$902,183

At the end of the 30 years, the policy expires. Does John need more? At this point, if he chose term life insurance and saved and invested the difference, he would have over $900,000 in investments! I could comfortably say that he no longer needs life insurance. He is now 'self-insured.' Congratulations Mr. Doe, you can retire with dignity!

I hope you now have a better understanding of the differences in whole life insurance and term life insurance. If you are convinced that by having a whole life policy, you are saving for your retirement, you insult your family. Instead, maximize your financial potential and give your family the gift of financial security by choosing term life insurance and keeping your investments and your insurance *separate*.

chapter five
The Costs of Home Ownership

Owning a home can save you money in rental costs. (Typically, a monthly mortgage payment is cheaper than a monthly rent payment.) In our area, with the current cost of renting, it made total sense for our family to buy a house. But, you have to be careful that the additional costs of being a homeowner don't kill your budget. The home we purchased was built in the 1950's, so it came with its own set of issues and repairs, each of which has cost us money. The last few years have provided us with some solid lessons in how to reduce these additional homeowner costs.

This next section is dedicated to home ownership. If you rent, some of these items may not apply yet. But, don't skip this section. There are many different ways that our "living expenses" can nickel and dime us, whether we own or rent our home or apartment. From cleaning supplies to taxes to heating and cooling costs, the living expenses are never ending. In the next few pages, we will talk about a few different homeowner tips for cutting costs and not letting the local contractor get the best of your budget.

Tip #23
Fix it Yourself

During our first year as homeowners, we had drain tile installed in our basement. (We came home to three inches of water in our basement after the first spring shower.) We also had to pay for some major electrical work, water heater repairs, HVAC repairs, lots of minor electrical repairs, and the list goes on.

It was bad. The local plumbing and heating/cooling systems repair company in town knew my husband on a first name basis. When he would call to request a repair, they didn't even have to ask for our address. We were regulars! And by being regulars, our budget was constantly taking the hit from repair fees.

We quickly learned that there are times where do-it-yourself YouTube videos are much cheaper than your local contractor! Having purchased a home with an unfinished basement and a home that needed quite a few updates, I can say today that we have done more than a few renovations over the last few years. Here's a short list of a few of the things we did...

~ Framed the entire basement.
~ Insulated the entire basement. (Bless my husband's heart.)
~ Installed laminate flooring.
~ Installed carpeting.
~ Installed a number of electrical components including a new thermostat, new light fixtures, light switches, electrical outlets, and a garage heater.
~ Installed 2 toilets, a bathroom sink/vanity, a new garbage disposal, a new faucet, and a dishwasher. (Yes, I have an awesome husband!)

~ Hung pocket doors.

~ And a million other little things!

Now, I'm not here to brag about all that we do. Rather, I am here to say that this took a lot of work on our part (and on the part of our friends and family) but it was totally doable (you can do it too) and saved us a ton of money!

You're probably wondering, how did we do all of this? (Because, let's face it, neither my husband or myself are trained in any trade fields.) The answer is simple: we learned. My dad taught us the basics of framing. We read step-by-step instruction books to complete certain projects. We watched videos by certified contractors on YouTube. And we gleaned advise from anyone who was willing to offer.

Now, I am not advocating that you do *all* renovations yourself. Trust me, there are definitely times to hire a professional. We hired professionals for a number of our bigger plumbing jobs and all of the electrical wiring work in our home was completed by a licensed electrician. However, when it comes to the smaller household repairs, check a home-repair reference book, Google, or YouTube to see if it is something you can handle on your own! It will save you money and the end result is pretty rewarding.

Side note: Fixing it yourself is not always much cheaper. If it involves purchasing a bunch of tools that you may only use once or paying to rent equipment, it may actually cost you more to fix it yourself. Be sure to weigh all of the factors. Oh, and don't forget to factor in your time. Time is a valuable commodity. If it's going to take you three days to complete a small home repair project, it may be worth paying a professional to get the job done in a couple of hours.

I want to take a moment to share a beautiful story with you – a story of a gift that my husband gave to me.

How many of you have a dishwasher? It's awesome, right? Well, when we bought our 1950's house three years ago, it didn't come with a dishwasher. At first, it wasn't bad. Then, we had one kid...and then another. Kids on top of daily life on top of major renovations...and, yeah, you guessed it...I was getting *way* behind with dishes.

So for my birthday this year, my husband gave me an awesome gift. He bought me a dishwasher! Now, the awesomeness of this gift doesn't end here. Let me explain...but, first, let's talk prices.

Do you know the average cost of a new dishwasher? About $400 to $700, with high-end dishwashers costing upwards of $1,000 to $2,000. How about the average cost of labor to have a dishwasher installed? On average, most homeowners pay $346 for installation.

Now, remember, I said the awesomeness didn't end with the purchase of the dishwasher. You see, my husband installed that dishwasher by himself. This involved cutting out a section of our cabinets, wiring a new outlet for the dishwasher, installing all of the plumbing to hook up the dishwasher, and securing the machine in place.

This was a huge gift. My husband took time to learn and to patiently work and re-work until he had that beautiful, shiny dishwasher installed. This gift didn't cost our family an extra $346 to hire a handyman, but it required a willing spirit on the part of my husband.

Tip #24

Pay Your Property Tax Early

In our town, you actually pay fifteen percent less on your property tax if you pay it before a certain date in February. Now, for our family this early bird discount is a difference of just under one hundred dollars. So, you can absolutely bet that each year we are prepared come February to pay early and save ourselves some money.

This is a fairly simple money-saving tip, but it does take a little bit of planning ahead. If you want to take advantage of this tip (that is, if your city offers an early bird discount on property taxes), I highly recommend you contact your city office to find out the early bird deadline and the discount percentage. Then, look back at what you have paid in previous years for property taxes, so you know what amount you will likely owe…subtracting the discount percentage, of course.

Start saving for this expense at least a couple months ahead of time, maybe more. How long you need to save completely depends on how much you can put away with each paycheck. Be sure to start saving with enough time, so that you will have the amount you need to pay your property tax before the early bird deadline.

Tip #25
Look into Refinancing Your Home

In the summer of 2015, interest rates were at an all time low, so we took advantage of the market and refinanced our home. When my husband originally purchased our home in 2014, he was fresh out of college and had a ton of debt. Now, despite debt and being a first-time home buyer, banks are usually willing to help out young people. However, it always costs you a bit more money in the form of interest rates. Sometimes, after a few years of good financial behavior, an increase in income, a decrease in debt, and a better credit score, you are eligible for a better deal (a lower interest rate).

There are two ways to look at refinancing as an option for saving money. The first way is to lower your monthly payment, thereby, decreasing the monthly expenses and increasing the monthly cash flow in your budget. Although this might 'save' you money in the short run, it may be the more expensive route to go. The second way, and the only reason I recommend refinancing, is if you can lower your interest rate. Changing the length of a term (For example, changing from a 30-year mortgage to a 15-year mortgage.) is mathematically a bad reason to refinance if your interest rate stays the same. Instead, simply pay more on your loan principal and you can pay off your loan in fifteen years. Refinancing costs money so if you can't lower your interest rate than don't spend the money.

In order to determine whether refinancing is an option for you, talk to a couple different mortgage companies. The more quotes you request, the more informed you will be and you will be able to pick the best rate. Shopping around pays! So, take time to check out of state, check online, and ask for references. Your lowest rate is not always going to be your local bank or the first online listing.

When considering whether or not to refinance, the first question to ask yourself: Is the new interest rate quote lower than your current rate? If yes, then you have an opportunity to save money by a refinancing. Once you know you can get a better rate, you need to determine your 'break even analysis'. That is, how long do you need to be at this new rate in order to save more money than you spent on the refinancing costs? This is a bunch of number crunching! Luckily there are a few calculators online that can help you out.

The table below outlines the basics. For this example, we are assuming that the cost of refinancing is $2,000 and is rolled into the loan. The cost break even calculates difference in payment, while the interest break even calculates interest payment savings.

	30-Year Original Loan	30-Year Fixed	15-Year Fixed & Lower %
Loan Amount	$100,000	$102,000*	$102,000*
% APR	6.250%	4.375%	4.375%
Payment	$615.72	$509.27	$773.79
Cost Break Even	---	19 mo.	---
Interest Break Even		14 mo.	13 mo.
Total Interest Paid	$121,658.19	$81,337.55	$37,282.69

When you get into a pool, the best way to get used to the water is to just jump in. If you are trying to save money by refinancing, go all in. The table above shows that, although a lower interest rate might decrease your payment, reducing the term will drastically change your interest paid. Even though the monthly payment on the 15-year fixed mortgage is higher, the loan is paid off fifteen years earlier. In the scenario above, refinancing would save the homeowner $84,000 over the life of the loan. That is $468 a month!

As I stated at the beginning of this tip we refinanced our home during the summer of 2015. Just three years later, during the summer of 2018, we sold our home as we sent off on our next life adventure. Thanks to our refinancing, we walked away with $4,700 more in our pockets!! Yes, in just three years, our refinancing had made a positive difference of $4,700 in the equity of our home. When I realized that our refinancing had made this much of a difference for our family, I found myself, once again, so thankful for my teammate on this adventure. Logan was proactive during that summer of 2015 and thanks to his actions, our family walked away with $4,700 more.

Tip #26

Colder in Winter and Warmer in Summer

I was raised on this 'colder in the winter and warmer in the summer' philosophy. My mom taught me...in the winter, you keep the thermostat slightly lower so you don't pay through the nose on heat. She taught me that you simply put on another layer, don some wool socks, or snuggle under a blanket. In the summer, it is just the contrary. You keep the thermostat slightly higher, as to avoid the high costs of running an air conditioner around the clock. If you're hot, you put on a tank top or open the windows at night when it cools down and shut the shades during the day to keep the sun heat out. By doing these two things, not only do you save money, but you also run a home that is more eco-friendly.

We have a thermostat that we love and it helps us to stick more closely to this colder in the winter and warmer in the summer philosophy. When we bought our house, my husband immediately replaced the old (very difficult to use) thermostat with a brand new smart thermostat. There are a number of advantages to using a smart thermostat.

First of all, we can set our smart thermostat to a schedule. For example, in the winter, in order to save on our heating bill, we let the house drop down to 64F at night. Our smart thermostat is preset for a schedule, so at 5:00 a.m., while we are still sleeping it bumps the temperature up to 68 degrees so that the house is warmed up by the time we get out of bed.

In the summer, it is just the opposite. We try to go without the air conditioning during the day. Usually if it isn't insanely hot and we keep some of the blinds closed, we can get away with this. However, at night we want our house to be cool, so we can sleep comfortably.

Our smart thermostat automatically starts dropping the temperature in the house to 68 degrees every night at about 6:00 p.m., a little over an hour before our girls go to bed.

Another feature that we love about our smart thermostat is our ability to control it from our phones. For example, typically we reduce the use of our air conditioning and heating when we are traveling. We allow our house to get down to 60 degrees or up to 80 degrees, by setting the thermostat to our preferred 'away' setting. If we leave for a trip and forget to change the thermostat to this 'away' setting, we can quickly make the adjustment from our phones!

I am not suggesting that you *have* to go out and buy the latest model of a smart thermostat. We made that investment because the thermostat that came with our house really didn't work well. Rather, I am suggesting that you keep an eye on your thermostat and be conscious about how much you are using your air conditioner or heater.

On the topic of energy usage and trying to make more eco-friendly, cost-effective choices, monitor all 'usage' in your home. When it comes to electrical usage, turn off lights. It's amazing how many lights can get turned on in our home and left on. Make sure you're not wasting electricity by illuminating rooms when no one is in them. If you have the space and the time, hang dry clothes or dry them partially in the dryer and then let them hang to finish drying. Don't leave the television on when no one is watching or the music playing when no one is listening. Additionally, be sure to unplug items when they are not in use. Even if you're not using at item, it is still drawing electricity when plugged in. So, keep things unplugged around your home. For example, when we aren't using them, our toaster and our Keurig are both immediately unplugged. No need to waste electricity!

I mentioned above monitoring *all* usage in your home. In addition to electricity, be conscious of how much water you and your family are using. Shorten shower times, don't leave the water running while you brush your teeth, be sure the dishwasher is full before running a load, and reduce the amount of water your toilet uses to flush (this can be done but adding a brick or a jug full of water or rocks to your toilet tank).

There are so many ways that our homes cost us money. Now, don't get me wrong, many of those costs are necessary. For example, if we didn't have heat in our home in the winter, not only would it be dangerous to live in our home, but it could also cause some serious (and expensive) damage when a pipe freezes and bursts. So, in summary, while these home costs are necessary, we may be over using and therefore over paying. Pay attention to the usage in your home and figure out if you can cut back in any areas.

Tip #27
Reusable Household Products

During our debt free journey, there were a few disposable household products that I realized I was paying way more for than necessary! And, to add to that, these products weren't good for the environment either. So, I made a few changes that have helped to cut our costs *and* reduce our environmental footprint.

Wool Dryer Balls

Towards the beginning of our debt-free journey, I purchased a set of six wool dryer balls from Amazon. There are a few benefits to wool dryer balls, including the following:

- *Reduce static.* Like the disposable dryer sheets I was accustomed to using, wool dryer balls help reduce static in your laundry.
- *Decrease drying time.* Wool dryer balls also aid in decreasing drying time, thus saving you the cost of additional electricity needed when not using wool dryer balls.
- *Can be used for many years.* These wool dryer balls last for years. This benefit is twofold – it saves the environment from the waste of throwing away disposable dryer sheets, and saves you the cost of having to buy disposable dryer sheets a few times every year.
- *Cloth diaper friendly.* For our family, wool dryer balls had one other key advantage…they can go in with our diaper laundry. When we wash cloth diapers, we bulk our loads with towels and washcloths. Cloth diapers cannot be dried

with disposable dryer sheets, so prior to discovering wool dryer balls our diaper and towel laundry was coming out full of static. I'm pretty sure I had to pry apart the towels!

I purchased a 6-pack of wool dryer balls on Amazon for just under $20. I do on average 6 loads of laundry per week including regular laundry and cloth diapers. That's about 312 loads every year! Before, switching to wool dryer balls, I was spending about $12 each year on dryer sheets. So, in less than two years, I have paid for the cost of my wool dryer balls!

I know individuals who have even made their own dryer balls, and some communities have local crafters who make and sell wool dryer balls. So, be sure to shop around and check all of your options before purchasing wool dryer balls!

Mop with Microfiber Cloth

When we began our debt-free journey, I was using a wet mop with disposable pads to clean our laminate floors. It did a fine job, but unfortunately it took three disposable pads to clean our laminate floors, which only included our entry, kitchen, dining room, and bathroom. When you have a toddler who leaves a mess of food on the floor after every meal and you end up mopping two to three times per week, using three wet pads per mopping gets expensive fast. I was spending almost one dollar *every time* I mopped!

So, partway through our debt-free journey, I made the switch. I started using a new mop – one that uses microfiber pads. In addition, it even has a sprayer, so it is tougher on those nasty kid messes. I purchased the mop at Walmart for about $20. I also purchased four microfiber pads that are for use with this type of mop. These microfiber pads are totally reusable – you just throw them in the laundry! (Side note: You wouldn't need four of these pads...that's just the number that worked best for our family with how often we mop our floors!)

Another perk of using this kind of mop is that you get to mix your own cleaning solution for the spray feature. I fill the sprayer compartment with water and one teaspoon of Pinesol (you can use the cleaner of your choice, but the mop company advises that you only use one teaspoon of cleaner…you don't need more than that). This mixture usually lasts me at least a month before I have to refill. And it is much cheaper than any pre-made solutions that you have to buy for so many mops.

If you are currently using a mop with disposable mop pads and/or a spray solution that you have to purchase specifically for that mop, but you are not ready to spend the money on a new mop, I have a couple of suggestions for you. Firstly, you can actually make your own reusable mop pads that will attach to your mop. There are lots of mom blogs out there with tutorials on how to do this. Secondly, although you have to buy specific bottles of spray solution to attach to numerous mops, on many of these mops there are tricks to refilling the spray bottle. A quick YouTube search will reveal whether or not you can refill your current mop spray solution bottle.

Gift Wrapping Items

We opt to reuse as many items as possible rather than throwing these things in the trash. For example, at Christmas time and birthdays, torn up wrapping paper is trashed. But tissue paper is smoothed out, bags and boxes folded, and bows gathered and saved for next year's Christmas and birthday presents. Not only does this cut down on holiday costs, it also keeps items that are still usable out of our landfills.

Plastic Easter Eggs

We save our plastic Easter eggs. I honestly didn't realize until this past Easter that there are many people who throw out their Easter eggs every year. I had been raised in a family who always, and still does, reuse their Easter eggs. I couldn't imagine it was done any other way, but I guess I was wrong. Our eggs are used year after year. An Easter egg is only thrown out when it is broken.

Spray Bottles

We also reuse spray bottles. There are so many products that come in spray bottles, including bathroom cleaners and laundry stain removers. Rather than throwing out perfectly good spray bottles, we save the spray bottle and buy a refill bottle of cleaner or stain remover (or whatever the product). Typically refill bottles come in larger sizes and cost less per ounce. Again, we are rewarded for buying in bulk!

Foaming Soap Dispensers

I have an affinity for foaming soap. I don't know why. I just prefer foaming soap. However, if you have visited your local store's hygiene section, you know that foaming soap is typically more expensive. As you may have already guessed, yes, I reuse my foaming soap dispensers! I keep a bottle of liquid hand soap in my closet. To refill my foaming soap dispensers, I simply fill with a solution of water and liquid hand soap.

Paper Products

Household paper products such as paper napkins and paper towels can be expensive (and fill up our landfills). While there are times that paper napkins or paper towels can be useful, there are many times that a washcloth, rag, or cloth napkin could be used instead. To save on paper products, we use cloth napkins during meal time. When cleaning, we almost always use washcloths and cloth rags rather than paper towels.

Ziploc Bags

We don't throw away our Ziploc bags after one use. Instead, we wash the bag and reuse it until it has a hole and is no longer usable. Only then is it thrown away. Trashing a Ziploc bag after one use is so wasteful and an expensive habit. If you want to take this tip one step further, you can make or buy your own reusable zippered baggies for all your snack and sandwich needs! These are a popular item right now among moms because they are easy to use, and they eliminate the wasted Ziploc bags (because we all know kids aren't necessarily gentle with their snack bags).

Do you best to analyze your routines. Look for items that you subconsciously toss in the garbage – items that could be reused or refilled in an effort to save you money and protect the environment. I've mentioned a few specific items on the last couple of pages that we have reused or refilled over the years. I am sure that there are countless other items that could be reused to cut costs and help save planet earth, so be creative as you implement this tip!

chapter six
Let Go of the Splurges

"I would die without my phone!" We've all heard this phrase. Some of us relate. Some of us don't. Chances are, in this day and age, it would be hard for you go without your phone. My husband and I each have a cell phone. We don't have a landline. He uses his phone for work; and I appreciate my phone with my stay-at-home business ventures. So, quite honestly, we wouldn't die without our phones, but it would seriously impair our ability to do our jobs.

Now my point is not to spend this next section discussing whether or not you would die without your phone. Instead, I want to challenge you to really evaluate the expenses of your lifestyle and see if you can find any 'splurges' that aren't really necessary. The next few pages will highlight a few of the splurges that we let go during our debt-free journey.

Tip #28
Reduce the Phone Bill

While our cell phones were a necessity, the amount of mobile data we were paying for was not. When my husband and I began our journey to become debt free, our cell phone plan included 6 GB of data per month. At that time, we felt that 6 GB was necessary as my husband was going to school, and this allowed him to do schoolwork while he was on the road. However, before we were done with our journey to pay off our debt, we were down to just 2 GB per month.

Cutting back to 2 GB per month was not hard for me. I am a stay-at-home mom, so I typically get along just fine on our household wireless internet, rarely using even 1 GB each month. However, for my husband, this took a little more determination to keep his data usage to just 1 GB per month. He was done with school, so he didn't have the same need for access to homework, but he had his fair share of work emails.

Here are a few tips from my husband to help you successfully cut down on data, even if you tend to be a bigger data user:

- ~ Turn off background data.
- ~ Connect to wireless internet anywhere that you possibly can – home, work, etc. Most public places have free wireless internet now so this is pretty easy to do!
- ~ Get rid of your smart phone altogether and go back to a dumb phone! They are cheaper, the batteries last longer, and you will be on your phone a whole lot less.

Another way to reduce your phone bill is to combine your plan with extended family members. The more phones that are on a plan, the less that you pay per phone. In my mom's family, my mom, both of her sisters, my grandma, and their family members share two phone plans between everyone. Because of the number of people on each phone plan, they pay less per phone.

Phones are an essential part of our society. However, just because your cell phone is a necessity, it doesn't necessarily mean that you and your family need, or actually use, the entirety of your phone plan. Analyze your phone bill. See how much of your plan you are actually using, and make adjustments accordingly.

Tip #29

No Cable – Stream Instead

Rather than paying high monthly fees for a local cable package (we are talking about $67.75 per month in our area), we opted to pay just $9 each month for Netflix.

I am not suggesting that you have to pay for Netflix. What I am suggesting is that, if you enjoy watching movies, television shows, or other media entertainment, you might want to look into options other than cable packages, which tend to be very expensive.

There are a number of streaming service companies that offer access to movies, television shows, or other media entertainment. This includes Netflix, Hulu, Amazon Prime, HBO NOW, Sling Television, and the list of possibilities goes on.

Don't forget to take advantage of events that are live streamed onto YouTube. Like I mentioned above, we don't have a cable package. However, my husband and I really enjoy watching big events such as the Macy's Thanksgiving Day Parade or the State of the Union. Well, thanks to many news companies who live stream some of these events onto YouTube, we have been able to watch the ball drop on New Year's Eve, follow the 2016 election results as Donald Trump's presidency began, and listen to some of the daily news.

Tip #30

No Eating Out. None.

Ok. So, it's not that we *never* ate out. We just didn't eat out if it meant we were going to pay for the meal.

Let me begin by explaining why we made the decision not to eat out. First of all, Dave Ramsey says that if you are in Baby Step 2 (the baby step that is dedicated to paying off your debt), then you are in no position to be eating out! You are in debt. You don't have the money to splurge.

Secondly, the cost of eating out was simply not worth it. One night about a year ago, we took our family of four (three was actually more accurate as our youngest daughter was fed baby food that we brought with us) to Applebee's for dinner. Our total? $31.30 plus a tip…and that's a lot lower than most 'eating out' bills. We took advantage of Applebee's 2 for $20 deal, used a free appetizer coupon, I drank just a water, and it was a Tuesday night (kids' night at Applebee's) so our oldest daughter's meal was just $0.99. Had we not been conscious of our choice of beverages and meals, we could have easily spent $50 for our little family to eat dinner.

Now, in the intro for this section, I mentioned that we just didn't eat out if it meant *we* were paying for it. What do I mean by this?

If one of our parents came to town and offered to take us out to eat, we didn't turn them down! We accepted this kind gesture and enjoyed having the opportunity to eat out. (My favorite part of eating out is that my kitchen stays clean!)

If you get the opportunity to eat out courtesy of your company's budget, take the opportunity! There were times that we enjoyed eating out thanks to my husband's company, and we had some of the best food.

If someone gives you a gift card to a restaurant, you should enjoy a dinner out! During our debt-free journey, our family got pretty smart. They started figuring out that when we were given any cash gift, we put that cash right on our debt. Their response? We started receiving gift cards instead of cash so that we had no choice but to slow down and enjoy a dinner out as a family.

Now, maybe you are like us, and you are debt free. You have gotten rid of all your debt and are once again enjoying the option of eating out on occasion. Can you eat out and still cut costs? Absolutely! Here are a few of my tips for those of you who want to eat out and save money on your restaurant bills.

Kids Eat Free

Many restaurants have a specific day or time of day dedicated to kids eating free. If you have kids, you likely know how expensive eating out can be for a family. Our family takes advantage of Applebee's Kids Eat Free Day (Tuesdays). With the purchase of one adult entrée, you receive a kid's meal for just $0.99 or $1.99, depending on the meal. Some restaurants also make special offers for other populations, including senior specials (for those over a specific age...this age varies by restaurant) or a reduced price for active military and retired veterans.

Restaurant Promotions

Many restaurants (including both sit-down restaurants and fast-food restaurants) offer a variety of promotions. These promotions can include a happy hour time (where certain beverages or food items are offered for reduced prices), a daily special, and a 2 for $20 deal (or something similar to this). Take advantage of these promotions!

My husband and I love Applebee's 2 for $20 and 2 for $25 promotions. We get one appetizer and two entrées for just $20 or $25 dollars, depending on the selected entrées. With a total of $20 or $25 plus a tip, this promotion lends itself for a much more reasonably priced date night.

Coupons

We have a number of schools and extracurricular groups in our community that fundraise by selling coupons. These coupons are good for use at certain local stores and/or restaurants. My husband and I sometimes take advantage of these coupon fundraisers. I say *sometimes* because before agreeing to purchase coupons, we make sure that they are coupons we will put to use. We don't want to spend money on coupons for restaurants where I can't indulge (I have food allergies that limit our choices). However, if the coupons being sold make sense for our family, we are typically happy to support whatever group happens to be selling them! And these coupons often have a great rate of return. For example, my husband recently purchased a sheet of coupons from the local softball team for just $20. This sheet contained coupons worth more than $100. What a great deal!

Apps

A number of restaurants have apps where they advertise current promotions, offer coupons or other deals, or reward points for purchases. If you are going to visit a restaurant, check to see whether or not they have an app.

When I downloaded the Dairy Queen app (DQ is a popular fast food and ice cream restaurant in our area), I received a free small blizzard. Since then, I have received coupon codes for a number of discounted food items. Another restaurant app on my phone is for HuHot. When I downloaded the app and signed up for HuHot Rewards, I was given a code for a free appetizer. In addition, the app tracks my purchases. For every 12 grill meal purchases, I receive one free grill meal.

Offers on Your Receipt

When you eat out, always check your receipt for any rewards being offered for your purchase. Many restaurants offer a free food item if you take a survey about your dining experience. By simply taking a five- to ten-minute survey about our dining experience, I have received rewards such as a free chicken sandwich from Chick Fil A, a free appetizer from HuHot, and $10 off a purchase of $20 or more at Pizza Hut. It pays to pay attention to your receipts!

When it comes to restaurants, if you are feeling totally and completely done being stuck in debt as we were, I encourage you to limit your eating out. If you really can't stand your debt (and it makes you mad), stop eating out altogether. Make it your mission to only go out to eat if someone else is paying – whether that be a dinner on the company or a gift card. However, if eating out is in your budget, please take advantage of some of our tips to cutting the costs of eating at a restaurant.

Tip #31
Cheap Date Nights

Although you might feel like I squashed your social life in the last tip, let me tell you that date nights can happen even on the tightest of budgets. And, I cannot stress enough, if you are in the middle of a debt-free journey, you NEED date nights…trust me! Why do I say this? Let me share a little story with you.

My husband and I worked together on this journey to become debt free. We worked hard for over two years to see this goal to completion. However, that hard work also meant long hours, days, and even (every once in awhile) weeks spent apart. When we did have free time, we typically spent that time at home where we were caring for kids, tending to chores, managing home repairs, and the list goes on. We didn't often go out with friends, and we were not partaking in many social activities as they required spending money.

This all being said, by the end of our debt free journey, we were feeling a bit lonely and isolated. For the past two years, we had been living like no one else – living a lifestyle so different from what society expects. This lifestyle had us focused on our goals, but left us feeling alone and withdrawn from the friends and activities we enjoyed.

So, for my husband and I, date nights were crucial. A date night meant we were getting time together, something that we highly treasured. It might mean that we were actually being a bit social (provided it was free or cost very little money). And it meant that for a couple hours we could just talk and dream together.

There were many times during our debt-free, work-like-crazy journey that it felt like during the few hours we were getting together, we were always discussing our debt or our budget. Our date nights were a time that we could really listen to our spouse's needs, and we could dream of our future plans together. Our date nights gave us hope for a future that would be different than our current lifestyle – a future that would include no debt, family vacations, a retirement savings bigger than I could imagine, date nights (that actually cost some money), school funding for our children, and most importantly, the power to give like crazy!

Thus, I say once again...date nights are important! So how, if you are in the process of paying off debt (or some other financial journey that is limiting your 'fun' money), can you partake in a date that won't cost $50 for just one night? Side note: I think we all know $50 is a low estimate. I mean, if my husband and I were to simply go out for dinner and a movie, with the cost of the babysitter for those four hours plus the cost of the date, it would be *well* over $50.

So, what can you do to keep your date night costs to a minimum? Here are some of my favorite suggestions:

Stay-At-Home Date
Sometimes the best dates are our dates snuggled up on our couch. Not only are they much cheaper, but they are usually enjoyed in our pajamas. Find a movie on Netflix for free or rent a movie from a rental company, grab some of your favorite snacks, and snuggle up! The cost of this date is just the price of the movie and the snack food, which is much cheaper than a trip to the movie theater!

Free Child Care
If you are a parent, you know that one of the most expensive

and stressful parts of any date night can be finding a babysitter for your children. If you have friends with kids, trade date night babysitting. You watch their kid(s) for a few hours so they can go on a date, and in return they do the same for you. Or if you have access to a grandparent, a family member, or a friend who loves kids and isn't worried about getting paid, take the opportunity to have a babysitter for free and enjoy an evening out with your spouse.

Community Events

Have you ever checked out the calendar of events for your community? (Most towns have an online calendar with a full listing of upcoming events.) If you haven't checked this out, I encourage you to do so! Our community's calendar is full of events including art showcases, art classes open to the public, concerts, fundraisers, celebrations of historic events, and the list goes on. Many of these events are free or come at a minimal cost. Check out what's going on in your community. You might be surprised at all the exciting happenings available for less than $10!

Enjoy the Outdoors

Nature is beautiful and it is free to enjoy! Take a stroll through the park, go dip your toes in a nearby lake, or have a picnic at the beach. These things are all free and can make for some very enjoyable quality time with your spouse!

DateBox

My friend recently introduced me to DateBox. I have yet to order an actual box, but from the free digital sampler they sent to my email and some research on their website (GetDateBox.com), I think this would make for a fun (and slightly cheaper) date night. DateBox is a subscription program. You subscribe and pay anywhere from $27.96 to $34.95 per month, depending on the subscription plan that you choose.

Once you subscribe, each month (around the 15th of the month) you receive a DateBox on your doorstep. The DateBox contains a variety of items that make a themed date to enjoy with your spouse or significant other. A few examples, as found on their website, include the following: a dance class DVD for dancing with your spouse and a bunch of ice cream toppings so you can enjoy a treat afterwards, a box full of Japanese items to use to make sushi together while listening to a provided Spotify playlist, or an adventure box with the ingredients for s'mores and stainless steel cups and a bag of the dried ingredients for tortilla soup. Most of these boxes also include some story or personal narrative with conversation starters and questions that you can enjoy discussing with your spouse or significant other.

When I started looking into the DateBox, I thought that $27.96 was kind of pricey, especially considering that sometimes you have to buy a few ingredients for the date night (DateBox provides you with a shopping list). However, when you consider that a night out can easily cost $50, DateBox would definitely be a little more cost-effective. I think another perk of ordering a DateBox would be that it simplifies your date night since everything is already planned. This ensures that you and your spouse can easily have some 'you time' without worrying about dinner reservations or finding a babysitter.

You need to be sure to take time to reconnect with your spouse. Having quality time together and investing in your relationship is important. You need the opportunity to dream together and remind one another of your goals, especially if you are in the middle of a challenging financial journey. I've provided you a few suggestions for cheap date nights. Get creative. Have fun with your spouse. And if you need more suggestions for low-cost date nights, consult Google or Pinterest.

Tip #32
Cancel Subscriptions

Have you looked at your bank statement recently? Do you really know where your money is going? It is amazing how many subscriptions you can forget about – subscriptions that are just being drawn out of your bank account on a monthly basis. So, sit down, sort through your bank account, and make sure that each transaction is accounted for.

Go through the subscriptions you do have. Do you need them? Do you use them? Is there a way to lower the rate? These are things you need to consider. If you aren't going to the gym because it's summer and you're spending time outside instead, then cancel your gym membership. If you have a random charge, then hunt it down!

While I was doing this, I found a charge for $2.99 that showed up once every three months. For years, this charge had been going on and I had no idea about it. It was such a small charge and the name on my statement was bland, not a company just some numbers and letters. When I looked up this charge online, I found multiple people looking for the same thing. It turns out that it was some PDF template I had purchased a few years before that had a hidden recurring fee for continued use of the template. It was very hard to track down and cancel. Last I heard, there was a pending lawsuit against it for being a scam. Once again, buyer beware!

Tip #33

Quit Buying Books – Get a Library Card Instead

If you are a book lover, you know that buying new books can get really expensive! Whether you are buying hard copy books, digital books on your tablet, or audiobooks from Audible, all of these options add up quickly. So, to save your budget from these book costs, I suggest getting a library card at your local library.

Most libraries offer library cards for no fee. We have a free membership at our local library. It allows us access to all of their books, audiobooks, and movies. In addition, we have access to resources from other libraries within our library's system.

If you enjoy having books on your phone, there are many libraries that also have eBooks and audiobooks you can check out. These books are usually checked out for a similar time period as that of regular books. However, the borrowing and returning of these books is all handled by an online program or app available through your library.

There are many ways you can reduce the cost of your book reading hobby. If you opt to buy a book, shop your local thrift store, shop used book sales (which are often hosted by local libraries or used book stores), or buy a used copy on Amazon or another site that sells used books. You can also host 'book exchanges' with your family and friends, where you all bring the books you've already read and exchange them for 'new-to-you' books.

If you are an avid reader but you want to reduce the costs associated with your hobby, be sure to check out your local library or consider other low-cost options before filling up your cart on Amazon.

Tip #34

Staycation Instead of Vacation

Vacations can be super expensive – the travel, lodging, food, and attraction expenses add up quickly. So, how do you have fun and relax with your family without paying the high price attached to so many vacation packages? Here are a few of our favorite tips:

Have a Staycation

Honestly, vacations are not always relaxing. The planning, the packing, and the traveling to your destination can all be quite hurried and stressful. Why not just ditch the stress and have a staycation instead? Stay at home and relax with your family! If you're really itching to get out, plan a small day-trip to a local lake, a picnic in the park, or a walk to the ice cream shop.

Take a Work Trip

My husband often travels for work. When his travels keep him within driving distance, the girls and I usually accompany him. We love it! My husband's company is already paying for his hotel room and the gas to drive there. So, I pack food (which takes a little bit of work, but keeps the costs lower), and we go with my husband. Although he has to work, the girls and I enjoy time relaxing in the hotel room or swimming in the pool, and the company takes care of many of the expenses of the trip.

Plan a Close-to-Home Vacation

The most expensive vacations are usually those that require a plane and a passport. So, why not plan a vacation close to home? Drive to a nearby city with a fun downtown life. Find a lower cost hotel or bed and breakfast and spend time exploring the town. Most local parks are free and window shopping downtown can be lots of fun!

Or, find a friend to visit. Bunk with your friend and spend time together. Or visit your nearest state park and pitch a tent! The fee for entry to state parks is typically very reasonable, and tenting is a low-cost option. You can spend time relaxing outdoors – hiking, fishing, or whatever you like.

Having time to slow down, relax, and enjoy your family is important, and a tight budget isn't reason enough not to enjoy a vacation. Do some creative thinking (or borrow one of my ideas from above) and plan a vacation that fits your budget!

chapter seven

Don't Feel Guilty: Holidays and Celebrations on a Budget

It's a fact…holidays can be insanely expensive. Christmas seems to come faster every year, and if you haven't been buying presents ahead of time, December can cause a real scare in your budget! The next small section is going to be dedicated to holidays, and what you can do to keep your favorite holiday festivity costs to an all-time minimum.

In addition to holidays, other life celebrations such as anniversaries, weddings, and birthdays can get expensive too. So, hang on for a few money-saving tips regarding these celebrations as well.

Tip #35
Keep Holidays Simple

It seems that every Christmas the pressure is on – pressure to have the perfect tree, the perfect decorations on your house and lawn, the perfect holiday party with the perfect treats, the perfect gifts, the perfect Christmas outfits for your children, and the 'perfect list' goes on. As if the pressure to have these things isn't enough, the expense to attain all of these things can be quite exorbitant.

Well, let me tell you...last time I checked, having the 'perfect everything' for Christmas didn't bring about more love or more joy. Rather, the love and joy of Christmas is found in the time spent with family and friends celebrating the true meaning of this holiday.

So, rather than spending your money to buy a full nativity set for your family's front lawn and tons of chocolate to make a mountain of Christmas treats, instead, simplify your holiday. Choose just one or two of your favorite treats to make. Forgo the lights on the house and the nativity in the yard. It will save you money on both the lights and decorations and the cost of electricity to light all of those decorations every night.

Our last Christmas before becoming debt free, we had a very little Christmas tree! It was a four-foot Christmas tree that we had purchased second hand the year before for just $5. When we purchased that tiny tree, we were hoping that we would have a full-size tree for the next Christmas.

Well, reality was that the next Christmas we were so dead set on being debt free by March that there was absolutely no room in our budget for a full-size Christmas tree. So, that Christmas we had our little four-foot Christmas tree yet again...but that wasn't all. That little Christmas tree was strung with one strand of colored lights with green wire and one strand of white lights with white wire. It was far from perfect!

Although our Christmas tree was quite a sight, we still had a beautiful Christmas! We had cherished time with our family – time decorating that little tree (and redecorating it at the end of every day after our almost two-year-old had successfully un-decorated it), singing Christmas songs, wrapping Christmas presents, eating Christmas treats, spending time with family, and best of all celebrating the story of Christmas. Those are the memories that matter! And truly, our girls will never remember our homely little Christmas tree.

Whatever the holiday – Christmas, Thanksgiving, Easter, Valentine's Day, the list goes on – try to simplify your holiday festivities. Do not give into the commercialism. Instead, appreciate the love of friends and family, and carry out a few simple traditions without breaking the bank.

Tip #36
Make Christmas Gifts

The last Christmas during our debt-free journey, we had a gift budget of $100. Yes, you heard me right...$100. That would need to buy Christmas gifts for our two girls, all four of our parents, three siblings (two with spouses, for whom we purchased joint gifts), one cousin, one aunt and uncle, and three nieces. While this is only a fraction of our family members, it still left us with 17 people to buy Christmas gifts for.

Now, I know you are probably doing the math by now...$100 to spend on 17 family members...that's just $5.88 per person. How do you buy a nice Christmas gift for a person with only $5.88 to spend on him or her? Well, you don't. I would say it's pretty near impossible to buy a nice gift for $5.88.

Now you're really wondering, how did we pull off this feat? We made almost all of our Christmas gifts. I am pretty sure the only thing we didn't make was one pair of dress shoes for our youngest daughter. Every other gift was homemade – painted welcome signs, decorative signs with quotes, marshmallow shooters, and sewn table runners and placemats. The reality is that paint, wood, fabric, and other supplies cost a lot less than buying brand new gifts.

Thus, by investing our time and talents (well, realistically *my* time and talents), we were able to spend just $100 on 17 family members. I will warn you that it took a lot of my time to make all of our Christmas gifts...and I may have had a meltdown...or two. If you decide to make your Christmas gifts, know that you will create gifts that will be loved by the recipients and you will save money, but it will take a hefty chunk of your time.

If you want to make your Christmas presents, but you are looking at my list of homemade gifts from above thinking…I can't paint, or I have never touched a sewing machine in my life…don't worry. First of all, I guarantee that you have gifts that I don't have – creative motives all your own. Second of all, if you are still convinced you lack all creative abilities, Pinterest and DIY videos are your best friends!

If you set your mind to having a low-budget Christmas, making your Christmas gifts is one of the best ways to cut costs and give gifts that are beautiful and meaningful!

Tip #37

Forget the Cards – Send Photos Instead

Let's face it, Christmas cards are expensive, especially when you have a family the size of Abraham's. With all of the online photo printing companies, it is easy to design your own Christmas card right from your couch! However, a nice Christmas photo card from Snapfish or Shutterfly on the conservative end costs $1 per card. Many of the card designs cost $2 or more.

We typically send out about 75 cards. (My husband's family really is the size of Abraham's...) At $2 per card, that is $150 just to purchase the cards, not including the shipping to get the cards to our home, AND the postage to mail out the cards to all of our family and friends.

So, this last Christmas, we took a new approach to Christmas cards. We wrote our usual Christmas letter, which was printed on basic computer paper. This is a very small expense – just some computer paper and printer ink – $5 at the most. However, rather than mailing this letter with a fancy card from Snapfish (our usual choice), we purchased some basic office envelopes from Walmart (about $5) and had 4x6 pictures of our family printed by Snapfish. We took advantage of one of Snapfish's Penny Print sales, where they offer 4x6 prints for just one penny per print. With the cost of 75 pictures and shipping, we paid less than $10 for our pictures.

Thus, in total our Christmas cards cost us about $20 plus postage this past Christmas...as compared to $150 plus postage. All of our family and friends still received a nice picture of our family and an update about our lives, but it didn't break our budget!

If you decide you want to eliminate your Christmas card expenses altogether, you could consider one of the following options. Rather than sending out a printed Christmas card and letter, you could send out an email with your family's update and a picture or an eCard. You could also opt to post your family's update along with a picture to Facebook. Be sure to consider all your options, giving thought to the best means to reach your family and friends, before choosing how to send this year's Christmas card.

There are many options when you are purchasing pictures – Snapfish, Shutterfly, and Walmart, to name just a few. Some of these photo companies, like Shutterfly, even offer free prints from their app. So, be sure to shop around and find the best deal before purchasing your family's Christmas photo.

Tip #38
Birthday Cards Instead of Gifts

Disclaimer: I am not at all suggesting that your child shouldn't get a birthday gift. I don't wish to cause your child scars for the rest of his or her life. So, please don't neglect your child's birthday. Just hear me out on this suggestion.

I am simply suggesting that you consider a few of the following cost-cutting tips when it comes to birthdays:

Give cards or moments instead of gifts.
There may be people on your usual birthday gift list that you could honor with a card filled with kind words or a gesture of kindness, rather than an expensive gift. My dad's birthday fell in the final month of our debt-free journey. Rather than buying him the latest grilling tool or golf accessory, we invited him to our house for the weekend of his birthday. We hosted him, made his favorite pasta dish for dinner, and topped off his birthday with a cherry custard complete with candles. He felt loved and celebrated without us breaking the bank on gifts.

Give a meaningful, low-cost gift.
If you know a person's love language, it is even easier to give them a very meaningful gift that doesn't cost a ton. If you don't know anything about love languages, here is a brief explanation so that I don't completely lose you. (A quick Google search will reveal more about love languages and allow you to take the love language test for yourself if you wish.) There are five love languages:

1) *Physical Touch* – Hugging, kissing, holding hands, a pat on the back, and other forms of expressing physical affection. This is very much a non-verbal love language, where you use your body to express love to another person instead of your wallet.

2) *Words of Affirmation* – Written or spoken words of encouragement that show affection. Speaking genuine words of encouragement often or sending an unexpected note both speak volumes to a person with this love language.

3) *Quality Time* – One-on-one time spent with another person – time that is free from distractions and interruptions. Spend time doing something together, but make sure your time is focused on each other (using eye contact when talking), in order to truly fulfill a person's need for quality time.

4) *Acts of Service* – Doing chores or completing tasks with the sole person of helping another person, thereby alleviating that person's workload. The phrase "What can I do to help you?" goes a long way with people who prefer this love language. Going out of your way to help with a task or completing a task together is a great way to express your love.

5) *Receiving Gifts* – Giving a meaningful gift. 'Meaningful' is the key word with this love language, as gifts must be thoughtful. Give a gift that matches this person or a gift that means something to them. No matter the size of the gift, the thoughtfulness behind

the gift will mean the world to this person.

We each have a certain way or ways (a love language) that we most appreciate love being spoken to us. In parallel, we tend to speak love to others in that same way.

For me, the two love languages I appreciate the most are Acts of Service and Quality Time. Knowing this, my husband could cook me dinner (an act of service) for my birthday, and then spend the evening playing a board game or sitting on the couch talking together (quality time). By doing this, he would make me feel very loved without hurting our budget at all.

While you do need all five love languages spoken to you, there tend to be certain languages that are more important for each person and some that are less important. For both my husband and I, receiving gifts is the last love language of importance. Thus, during our debt-free journey, we very rarely gave each other gifts. We pretty much gave one gift at Christmas and that was it! The way we saw it…giving gifts was an unnecessary expense and we were able to love each other in different ways.

If you know the love languages of those closest to you, try to use that knowledge to give 'gifts' of love – gifts that speak love to the other person, but don't cost as much. Side note: This tip is better for giving gifts to adults. Most kids still really want a present on their birthdays.

Think twice about your kid's gift.
That being said, let's talk about kids. If you are trying to cut costs, please think about what you are planning on giving your child for his or her birthday. I am sometimes appalled at size and quantity and price of gifts that are given to children. For example, does your eight-year-old really need the latest version of the iPod? Probably not. In addition, your eight-

year-old is likely not ready to treat a gift of that expense with the respect that it should be given. Thus, really give thought to a gift for your child. Don't buy them the latest expensive gadget just because that's what everyone else is doing. Give a gift that matches your child's interests and makes sense for his or her level of maturity.

With both Christmas and birthdays, we keep gifts for our girls very simple...and they LOVE it! For example, when our oldest daughter celebrated her second birthday, she received two gifts. Together these gifts only cost about $14. My husband and I gave her a t-shirt with fish on it (fish are her favorite animal, so she loves this shirt), and a fishing pole (which was such a hit she didn't actually eat any of her birthday cake...not a single bite).

Think about the money you are spending on birthdays. Buying smaller gifts, sending cards, and doing something for someone (an act of service) rather than buying something are all ways to celebrate birthdays without spending your hard earned cash.

Before I close this chapter on gifts and holiday celebrations, I want to tell you a story from a recent Mother's Day.

In honor of Mother's Day (the Mother's Day that fell just a couple months after the conclusion of our debt-free journey) Logan and the girls sent me a bouquet of pink and orange flowers. The flowers were absolutely gorgeous!

But, they were so much more than that. You see, Logan and I had been married for over three years and those were the first flowers I had ever received. Now, you might be thinking...*how unloving of him never to send me flowers in three years*. However, that lack of flowers was truly an act of love. An act of love and dedication.

Logan really likes giving gifts, and he would have loved to bring home a bouquet of flowers for every special occasion and "just because." So, it took self control and willingness on his part to stick to a tight budget even though he wanted to give his wife more. Instead, he found other ways to speak love to me.

So, that Mother's Day, those flowers were more than just gorgeous. They meant more than just 'thank you' and 'happy Mother's Day.' They were yet another symbol of achieving our debt free goal. I am so incredibly blessed; and I am thankful that my husband was willing to honor our journey and wait until that day to bless me with flowers.

chapter eight
Rapid Fire: Bonus Tips for Slashing Costs

Thus far, we have discussed a number of different ways to cut costs in specific budget areas such as kids, food, holidays, etc. However, there are also things you can do to cut costs as a whole. These tips affect many different items in your budget from the kind of coffee or food you buy to the household cleaners and diapers that are filling your cart.

This next section is dedicated to a few of these more 'all-encompassing' tricks. Hold on! We are about to take the reins on multiple areas of your budget.

Tip #39

Buy the Generic Brand

Have you noticed how much more we pay sometimes just for a certain name? Let's talk about what we can do to avoid paying high prices for brand name products.

One of the more expensive brand name items that we were purchasing for the longest time was Zyrtec. I have allergies and I take Zyrtec on a daily basis. During the worst of allergy season, I even take it twice a day. My point…I go through a *lot* of Zyrtec!

Now, here's a little lesson for you…when it comes to medications, typically there is a generic brand option that has the *exact same* active ingredient (meaning, it treats the same symptoms) as the brand name option. However, the generic brand medication costs a fraction of the cost of the brand name medication. In the case of Zyrtec, we found that there is another option. The active ingredient in Zyrtec is known as Cetirizine. For example, Walmart carries Zyrtec. They also carry a generic brand allergy medication called Equate Allergy Relief. It contains the exact same amount of Cetirizine as Zyrtec, but costs quite a bit less!

Because this allergy medication is something that I use at least once a day, we buy it in bulk at Sam's Club. (This is one of those times where buying in bulk makes sense as the item will not expire before I use it.) And buying in bulk saves us even more money. Sam's Club also offers a generic allergy relief medication with Cetirizine and it costs significantly less than Walmart's generic brand Cetirizine.

Medications are not the only products that have generic options. Generic brand products are everywhere! There are generic brand options for most hygiene products, household cleaners, food products, baby items, and the list goes on and on.

Now, I understand that there are times when you may want the brand name product because it is higher quality. (We buy name brand Tide laundry detergent because, for our laundering needs, it works so much better than other detergents.) However, there are many times that the generic brand product is just as good and just as usable as the brand name product. So, the next time you are shopping, I encourage you to really search the shelves. Take note of how often you are paying more just for a name. See if any of the brand name products in your cart could be replaced with a generic brand product.

Buying generic brand products can cut down immensely on your grocery budget. To showcase these savings, I shopped at Cashwise (one of our town's grocery stores) for three dinners for a family of four. I compared generic brand and name brand (tax not included). Here were my findings:

Dinner #1: Hearty Beef Chili

Ingredients	Generic Price	Name Brand Price
Ground Beef 80% (16 oz.)	$3.48	$4.48
Onion (1)	$0.71	$0.71
Green Bell Pepper (1)	$0.77	$0.77
Chili Beans (2 cans, 15 oz. each)	$1.50	$2.98
Great Northern Beans (1 can, 15 oz.)	$0.75	$1.19
Tomato Sauce (1 can, 15 oz.)	$0.88	$1.25
Diced Tomatoes (1 can, 28 oz)	$1.68	$2.48
Chili powder	$0.50	$0.74
Total:	**$10.27**	**$14.60**

Dinner #2: Barbeque Chicken and Vegetables with Rice

Ingredients	Generic Price	Name Brand Price
Boneless Chicken Breasts (16 oz.)	$1.99	$3.55
Onion (1)	$0.71	$0.71
Green Bell Peppers (2)	$1.54	$1.54
Mixed Frozen Vegetables (1 bag, 16 oz.)	$1.98	$3.39
Tomato Sauce (1 can, 15 oz.)	$0.88	$1.25
Barbeque Sauce (1 bottle, 18 oz.)	$1.68	$2.21
Brown Sugar	$0.05	$0.07
Total:	**$8.83**	**$12.72**

Dinner #3: Spaghetti

Ingredients	Generic Price	Name Brand Price
Ground Beef 80% (16 oz.)	$3.48	$4.48
Onion (1)	$0.71	$0.71
Spaghetti Noodles (16 oz.)	$1.18	$1.59
Spaghetti Sauce (1 jar,	$1.25	$2.13
Total:	**$6.62**	**$8.91**

Comparing these three dinners, you can see that I saved between $2.29 and $4.33 by purchasing generic items rather than name brand products. This might not seem like a big deal – it's only a few dollars, right? Well, if we take the average amount saved on these three dinners and consider cooking one dinner per day for an entire month, you will save about $105 each month by purchasing store brand products! Now, saving $105 per month (saving $1,260 per year) – that's a big deal!

I sure hope that I have convinced you to try generic brand products. While the savings per meal may seem small, over time this is a tip that will save you big bucks! Next time you go to the store, look over the shelves from top to bottom. Don't grab a product just because that's what you always buy. Rather, consider buying store brand products to lower your grocery bill!

Tip #40

Use Everything in Your Cupboards

From random cans of soup to countless tiny, half-used bottles of shampoo from hotels, we all have things in our pantries and our cupboards that have been sitting there for months (ok, maybe years). So, take advantage of these forgotten food and hygiene products to avoid spending money on new products.

There were times during our debt-free journey that my husband or I would open up the kitchen cupboards and just start Googling the random ingredients left in our cupboards. This may sound strange, but typically Google came up with some tasty recipe for us to make with the ingredients. Many times, this would get us through another dinner or two before having to buy groceries. It also helped us use up some of those items in the back of our cupboards that were close to expiring.

If you are meal planning for the next couple of weeks, look in your cupboards before you start planning. There is no point in buying more food items at the grocery store if there are usable items sitting on your shelves. So, plan some recipes that will use items you already have!

This adventure of using everything in your cupboards is not limited to the food items in your kitchen. Think about your bathroom drawers. How many times do we buy a bottle of shampoo and use half of it, before setting it aside and buying another? Or how about your cleaning closet? How many bottles of half-used cleaners (that are still perfectly good) have been pushed to the back and forgotten?

Scour your cupboards and closets. Use the forgotten, half-used products that are just sitting there. Use the little shampoo and lotion samples that you have carried home from every hotel. Side note: I am pretty sure we could last at least two or three months using products from our 'samples drawer' for our hygiene needs. By using these long-forgotten products, you will use items that would have otherwise gone to waste *and* save yourself money by not buying a new product until you actually need it.

Tip #41

Buy in Bulk…Sometimes

There are times for buying in bulk…and there are times for not. As I mentioned in a previous tip, for me, buying my allergy medication in bulk was a huge money-saver, but that is not the case with all products. First, let's talk about when buying in bulk makes sense:

You use a large amount of this product.
I use my allergy medication on at least a daily basis, and I don't foresee discontinuing the use of this medication any time soon. Thus, there is no reason I won't use a large amount of allergy medication, so it makes sense to purchase this product in bulk.

The product will be used before expiring.
I am more than capable of finishing a large bottle of allergy medication before it expires. However, if buying in bulk means that the product you are buying is going to expire before you are able to use it, then buying in bulk is a waste and does not make sense.

It is a cost-cutter.
Buying in bulk is a huge cost-cutter when it comes to my allergy medication. It's a difference of almost $49 every year! So, if buying in bulk is a relief for your budget, go for it!

However, there are times that buying in bulk does not save you money in the long-run, and therefore is not a good idea. Next, let's talk about times to avoid buying in bulk:

The product will expire.
If you run the risk of the product expiring before you can use it all, then buying in bulk is a wasteful option – it wastes the product itself and it wastes your money. For example, with our first child, I bought big containers of baby cereal. She never even used half of the baby cereal that I purchased. Eventually the cereal was thrown. It had expired and could not saved for baby number two.

The product will not be used.
Even if the product isn't going to expire, if you are not going to be able to use all of the product, buying in bulk is a waste. For example, we are getting ready to move; and we don't want to have to move a bunch of food, cleaning, and hygiene products. That means I am buying less products in bulk, so that we don't have to throw products when it comes time to move.

While buying in bulk may appear to be cheaper, consider all the pointers highlighted in this tip before buying a product in bulk. A few examples of other items I tend to buy in bulk include dish soap, laundry detergent, stain remover, toilet paper, hand soap and lotion, shampoo, and other such products that I know we will use and that won't expire.

Tip #42

Get Amazon Prime…If It Pays

If you live in a small town where you can't get your hands on certain products without paying crazy high prices, or if you typically purchase products online, then Amazon Prime may be worth it for you! Carefully weigh the cost of an Amazon Prime membership and the money saved before deciding whether it makes sense for you.

To begin, let's talk about the cost. Amazon Prime is available at a cost of $33 for three months or $99 for twelve months. Amazon Prime members enjoy the following benefits, as outlined on Amazon.com[1]: free two-day shipping on any Amazon Prime item (this includes over 50 million items), access to Prime Video (which allows you to watch thousands of movies and television shows), millions of songs and thousands of playlists available for streaming, free Kindle eBooks, unlimited photo storage, exclusive access to deals, Twitch (with includes access to bonus video games and exclusive in-game content), and much, much more.

To be honest, the only benefits of Amazon Prime that we really use are free two-day shipping and Prime Video (which we use to rent movies every once in awhile). Funny enough, as I was writing this section, I started to realize that maybe Amazon Prime is not the most cost-effective option for our family at this time.

In discussing this with my husband, we found that we really weren't making up for the $99 we were paying every year. Formerly, it was the lack of shipping costs that made up for the $99 we paid for our membership. But, lately we haven't been making as many online purchases. Realizing this, I suggested that we buy three months of Amazon Prime for $33 around November. That would cover us for the Christmas season, helping us save on shipping costs when we need it most.

So, the moral of my story? The little realization I had proves that it is worth it to look into your expenses often. Just because paying for a service, such as Amazon Prime, was saving you money at one point doesn't mean that it will always be most cost-effective. Analyze your expenses often so you can ensure that you are using your money (well, God's money) wisely.

Tip #43

Get a Sam's or Costco Membership

Like Amazon Prime, a membership to Sam's Club or Costco may be a benefit. However, if you don't need any of the products that these club memberships offer, then the savings will not outweigh the cost of the membership. Before paying for access to one of these clubs, you will want to do a little research and seriously consider whether it is beneficial for you and your family.

Now, I am going to speak specifically about Sam's Club because that is the membership that we have. However, if you are looking at a membership, check out Costco as well and compare which store will be best option for your family. Let me explain a little bit about Sam's Club...

The most basic Sam's Club Membership, called Sam's Savings, is available for $45 per year. The Sam's Plus plan, which includes more benefits, is available for $100 per year. We choose to buy the Sam's Savings membership, as we don't feel we need to access the additional benefits available with the Sam's Plus membership plan. A full listing of the memberships and their corresponding benefits are available on the Sam's Club website.

How do you know if a Sam's Club Membership is right for you? Well, it's simple. If you can save more than $45 by shopping at Sam's Club, then your membership is worth it! If you don't save more than $45 by shopping at Sam's Club, then you are wasting money on the membership fees. Here's how I justify our Sam's Club membership...

Generic Brand Medication

As I previously explained, I take a generic brand medication called Cetirizine for my allergies. At Sam's Club, I can buy a

400-count bottle of Cetirizine for about $15-17 plus tax, sometimes less if it is on an Instant Savings special (these are sales run by Sam's Club). This bottle is enough to get me through almost one year!

At Walmart, I can buy Equate Cetirizine (again, the generic form of this medication) at the price of $29.86 plus tax for a bottle that contains only 180 tablets. That means, if I were to buy 400 Cetirizine tablets at Walmart, it would cost me about $66.36 plus tax. So, by choosing to buy my allergy medication at Sam's Club, I save right around $49 per year. That purchase alone justifies my family having a Sam's Club membership!

Side note: I recently discovered that Walmart has started selling a generic brand Cetirizine online that is much more comparable to the cost of what I buy at Sam's Club. However, because this is not the only item we save on at Sam's Club, a membership is still beneficial for our family.

Low-Cost Produce

I buy almost all of the strawberries and blueberries that I freeze during the summer season from Sam's Club. I not only save money on my produce, but I find that Sam's Club almost always offers higher quality fruit than our local grocery stores.

Lower Milk Prices

We also often take advantage of the lower milk prices that Sam's Club offers. Now, the closest Sam's Club to where we live is about 90 miles away, so we are not going to drive to Sam's Club *just* for milk. But, if we are already planning to be in a city with a Sam's Club, you can bet that we will purchase some lower-priced milk while we are there!

I want to highlight just one more thing that I love (I mean, really love) about Sam's Club. They offer Store Pick-up. If you are a mom of young kids, like myself, you are going to love this too. Here's how Store Pick-up works…I go online and do all of my shopping at whatever hour of the day (most of the time, I am in my pajamas on the couch placing an order). When I checkout, I designate a day and time that I would like to pick up my order. I go to the store at this designated time, walk in and show them my membership card, and they bring out a cart filled with all of my goodies, which I already paid for online. My shopping is done, so it's one less store that I have to tackle with kids in tow! I love the ease that Store Pickup offers.

Whether you enjoy baking for your family, like to have healthy snacks such as nuts and dried fruit, or simply have a big family that you are trying to feed, I encourage you to look into getting Sam's Club or Costco membership. Chances are, you will find some great savings! Just remember, before you buy in bulk at either of these clubs, be sure you are actually going to use the product before it expires.

Tip #44

Do Your Research – Shop Around

Whenever I have a new item to buy, especially a bigger ticket item, I don't just go to Walmart and buy the first thing I see. Instead, I shop around. Before even stepping into a store, I prepare by doing some online research.

It's amazing what a quick Google search can reveal. You can easily take a look at the different companies that sell that specific item. You can read reviews to find out which brand or model is the best. You can compare prices of these different models, and prices offered by different stores.

By completing a quick Google search, I not only know more details about this product, but I have typically come to a conclusion about where to buy such item, unless there is a local store that I want to check before buying.

By conducting my online research and shopping around, I have saved myself from buying a product that won't last (reviews are a big help when deciding if a cheaper product is worth it), and saved myself from spending more on an item than necessary.

There have been many times when, in searching for a product, I have found the most cost-effective option on Amazon. Since we have Amazon Prime and receive free 2-day shipping, I obviously choose to buy the product from Amazon because I am more than willing to wait two days in order to save some money.

In order to ensure that you are spending your money wisely and cutting costs where it makes sense, I encourage you to use the internet to your advantage. The internet makes it simple to thoroughly research new products before buying and to find the most cost-effective option.

Tip #45
Check Your Routines

Do you stop every morning on your way to work to pick up that piping hot cup of Starbucks coffee? Or do you make a trip to the candy or pop machine on your work breaks? Or do you make a habit of always buying the Amazon daily deal? Take a look at your daily routines. What is included in that routine? Do you perhaps have what is known as a "Latte Factor"?

The "Latte Factor" was a term made popular by the financial expert David Bach. According to the official website of David Bach, "The Latte Factor® is based on the simple idea that all you need to do to finish rich is to look at the small things you spend your money on every day and see whether you could redirect that spending to yourself. Putting aside as little as a few dollars a day for your future rather than spending it on little purchases such as lattes, bottled water, fast food, cigarettes, magazines and so on, can really make a difference between accumulating wealth and living paycheck to paycheck."[1]

Let's take one of our hypothetical questions from above – that morning cup of joe from Starbucks. For this example, we will assume that you stop every morning before work to get your Starbucks coffee. That is about $5.00 every morning. At five business days per week (assuming you don't grab coffee on the weekends), that is $25 per week – that's $1,300 per year! Just in coffee!

If you were to simply take that $25 per week and invest it instead in an account with an annual interest rate of 10 percent, in 40 years (from *just* $25 per week…that's pocket change for you!), you would have over $685,503.88. If you increase that interest rate to 12 percent, you're now looking at a total of more than 1.2 million dollars. Woah!

Is your daily morning coffee really worth giving up that much in retirement savings? It sounds to me that if a few more people were willing to buy that $6 tin of coffee at the grocery and make their coffee at home, we might have quite a few more millionaires in this country!

Our routines – our habits – are so commonplace in our minds and our schedules that it's easy to not even realize you are spending that money! Before my husband and I got married, he began analyzing his bank statements looking for his Latte Factor. At the time, he was working as a full-time paramedic. Our local ambulance commonly transfers patients 90 miles either east or west to a larger hospital. After dropping off the patient, it is habit for the ambulance crew to stop at the gas station to get fuel and snacks before making the return trip.

So, what was my husband's Latte Factor? His gas station snacks – corn dogs, hotdogs, coffee, chips, you name it! He was spending about $70 every month on food at gas stations. That's approximately $2 to $3 every day. Translating that instead into retirement savings with 10 percent interest rate? The result after 40 years is about $355,401.82 (investing $2 per day) to $533,102.73 (investing $3 per day).

I think I've made my point. Your Latte Factor could be costing you the retirement of your dreams. However, if somehow I haven't yet convinced you or I have convinced you and you want more information about how to identify and combat your Latte Factor, I highly suggest you check out David Bach. He has an official website, as mentioned above, with all kinds of great resources including a blog, numerous books, and the 'Start Late – Finish Rich' Class.

So, what did my husband do to avoid his Latte Factor (gas station food)? He began making sure his backpack and his locker at work were stocked with snacks and food that he could grab on the go. If he was working long hours and needed some caffeine to stay awake, he took coffee from work on the road or took his 'free refill gas station mug' with him. And, as his wife, I helped and encouraged him as he worked on changing this habit. I packed him meals to take to work, delivered him meals at work when he was kept working long hours, and held him accountable if I noticed any gas station charges on our account. Logan avoiding his Latte Factor took a little more work and planning ahead, but he was dedicated to getting his family out of debt and making healthier food choices for himself, both of which helped him to avoid his Latte Factor.

Tip #46
Re-evaluate Your IRS Withholdings

I am going to say something that might take your breath away. Every paycheck you get has money removed from it by the Internal Revenue Service (IRS). Often times, the government will take too much money from your paycheck. This is money you could be using to buy food, pay off debt, or put towards your retirement. How do you know if they are taking too much? That's easy enough to answer. Do you get a tax refund in the spring? The refund is essentially the government reimbursing you for taking too much.

While some see this as a nice way to give yourself a cushion every spring, it is not. I see it as a short-term loan given to the government that is paid back with no interest. Allow me to change your mind. Your goal is to *not* get a refund! You want to give them exactly what they require; nothing more, nothing less. Santa Clause does not live in Washington, DC, and that is not a gift you are getting. It is money you receive because of a lack of math on your part. You must get a handle on it!

You are allowed to claim dependents on your W2 even if you don't have kids. Use that to your advantage to increase or decrease the amount that is going to be taken off of your checks. The IRS tax tables are not the greatest and you need to do a little pencil pushing in order to hone in on the proper withholding. Luckily, the calculation is fairly simple.

Take the amount of your refund and divide it by twelve months. Take that dollar number and figure out how many dependents you need to claim in order to make up that difference. Work with your payroll department or HR in order to figure out your withholding. Don't go crazy with this or you will get a bill in the spring. We don't want that either. Use this tip to immediately see a change in your take home pay.

Tip #47

Do Not Buy New Clothes

Luckily, once we are adults, we don't do as much growing. (Hopefully we don't grow anyway because most growing seems to be out and not up.) Because of this, we don't require nearly as many clothes as those growing toddlers and teens. Therefore, I strongly encourage you to cut down on your costs by avoiding buying new clothes for yourself and your spouse.

By the end of our debt-free journey, I had been through two pregnancies and there were many pairs of jeans that I was simply never going to fit into again. The two pair of jeans that still fit had been with me since my sophomore year of college. Thanks to the wear and tear of daily life, within a couple of months following the birth of our second daughter, I popped the buttons on both pair of jeans. The worn denim fabric was ripped with no hope of holding a button again.

Now, for most people that would have been the final straw, and a new pair of jeans would be considered a necessity. However, we were within four months of our debt-free goal; and I was too stubborn. There was no way I was going to spend money on myself when we were that close to achieving our goal. So, for a few months (until God blessed me with two JCPenney gift cards from a couple of friends) my only two pair of jeans were each held together with a hair tie. Please don't ask about the logistics. It was complicated.

If you find yourself in a situation where clothes are an absolute necessity (maybe you are pregnant and have no work-appropriate clothes that fit), I still encourage you…do not buy *new* clothes. Scour your local thrift stores and garage sales, or borrow maternity clothes from a friend. Host a clothing swap with your friends. When you host a clothing swap, you get together with your friends and each person brings clothing items from their closets that they no longer want. You then freely swap the unwanted clothes and everyone walks away with new treasures at absolutely no cost! Trust me, from garage sales to clothing swaps, there are ways to get nice clothes for a lot less than in-store prices.

chapter nine
Giving on a Budget

There is one last topic I want to explore before sending you on your way to begin cutting costs. I don't know about you, but my husband and I have pretty big hearts. When we hear of a friend who is struggling or someone who has a need, it's hard not to want to give…it's hard not to fill that need. So, how did we approach these giving opportunities amidst our debt-free journey? How did we continue to serve and continue to give during a time when we didn't have money to spare?

Just a side note before we start this section…I am not suggesting that you eliminate all financial giving in your budget. We didn't. We felt convicted that no matter our financial situation, we always needed to tithe. Why did we feel this way?

Well, first and foremost we are instructed by the Bible to tithe. According to Leviticus 27:30, "A tenth of the produce of the land, whether grain or fruit, is the Lord's, and is holy." In Nehemiah 10:35, Nehemiah instructs the Levites, "We obligate ourselves to bring the firstfruits of our ground and the firstfruits of all fruit of every tree, year by year, to the house of the Lord." We are reminded of this again in

Proverbs 3:9-10, "Honor the Lord with your wealth and with the firstfruits of all your produce; then your barns will be filled with plenty, and your vats will be bursting with wine." We are supposed to give the first part of our income to the Lord. In fact, we are "obligated" to give first to Him! So, on our budget, our tithe is the very first category.

By tithing before anything else, we keep God at the forefront of our lives. Consistent tithing has instilled in us the importance of giving, reminding us to live unselfishly. I believe this is preparing us to be give more as we are blessed with more, always reminding us to use our income to further God's kingdom here on earth.

Second, this money that we have is not ours, but rather a gift from God. He has blessed us with opportunities for income, and given us strong bodies and able minds to be able to carry out the work He has asked us to do. Therefore, because God has blessed us so richly, we feel it is of utmost importance to give the first portion of our income back to Him.

In this next section, when I talk about not having the money to give, I am referring to the supplemental giving (beyond tithing) that we felt called to do. So, let me share some of the ways that we were able to give without diverting our attention from the debt-free journey God had called us on.

Tip #48
Provide a Meal

I can't tell you how much it means to have someone offer to bring you a meal in the chaos of life. Do you know a new mother or someone who recently lost a close family member? Or maybe one of your friend's spouses is traveling for work and your friend is trying to take care of their kids for a week by him or herself? Or maybe you know someone – a friend, a family member, or just an acquaintance – to whom you would like to show love. Take a meal to this person!

It probably makes a difference that one of my top love languages is Acts of Service, but I can tell you that when a few of our friends offered to bring a meal following the birth of our second daughter, it meant so much to me! I felt, since this was our second child, that I should just know how things go. I mean, I had done this before, hadn't I? I really thought I should just have everything together.

Can you say reality check? Reality was, our second child was completely different than our first (what a surprise!). Her personality was different, she struggled with acid reflux, and sleeping was complicated because she was in so much pain. Reality was, for the first two months of her life, I got about three hours of sleep per night. I didn't have everything together. I was doing my very best to take care of our new baby and still give our toddler the time and attention that she yearned for, but many days I felt like I was failing.

Offering to bring a meal might seem like a simple act, but for me, as a new mom, it meant a night off from cooking. It meant no evening meal prep, which also meant I could take an afternoon nap. A meal usually resulted in leftovers, because our family is small, which also meant that lunch was taken care of for the next day. This simple gesture was a big deal in my crazy world!

Not only is a meal the perfect way to say 'I love you,' or 'We are thinking of you,' but it is also a low-cost way to give to someone around you. This gift requires a bit of grocery money and a little more of your time, because if you're looking to give a low-cost gift, it means cooking rather than just picking up a meal at the local caterer.

Now, what if your budget is at a point that you can't afford to make an entire meal? That's ok. Think muffins! Muffins are easy to make and require very few ingredients, most of which the average person has on hand in their pantry.

I can't tell you how many times I delivered muffins to friends who needed some love, because quite frankly, we couldn't afford anything else. Through those simple muffins, I spoke love. I prayed while I mixed and baked, I wrote a brief note, and then I made my delivery (many time anonymously). Moments making muffins for friends of ours are moments that filled me up and lifted my spirit as I had the opportunity to give.

Never doubt your ability to give. As Mother Teresa once said, "If you can't feed a hundred, feed one." While your budget might not allow you to feed a village in a third world country, a few ingredients in your cupboard used to create a simple treat or a meal for a grieving family. Your gift of cooking may be exactly what someone needs today.

I want to take a moment to share a beautiful story with you – a story that speaks to this style of giving. This took place the during our first summer living debt free. Little did I know, as I prepared those meals or those muffins, I was not only impacting the people to whom we gave, but I was also writing on the heart of our daughter.

Some time ago I was backing out of the driveway to go run a few errands. All of a sudden, our two-and-a-half-year-old piped up from the backseat. "Momma," she said, "Take food?"

You see, she knew we were headed somewhere and she wanted to know if we were going to deliver a meal to someone in need.

I have to admit, in the past few years, there have been many moments as a mom where I have just paused and admired my beautiful girls, soaked up a memory, and thanked God for my time with them. But, this one moment dropped me to my knees…figuratively, of course, since I was trying to drive.

I remember stopping the car. Just halting. I was overcome by the question my toddler had just posed.

I mean, we hear things like, "More is caught than taught." And we strive as parents to model the love of Christ. But that's a *really BIG* job. The love of Christ is no small thing. And while I want to model that every moment of every day, I know full well that amidst the tantrums, tangles, and tears of everyday life, I fall short.

So, when my toddler said, "Momma, take food?" I just stopped. Tears welled in my eyes as I thanked God. The love of Christ that I work so hard to model, despite my imperfections, had come full circle. My daughter, at two and a half, had already recognized the importance of providing for those in need.

I stopped. I prayed. I thanked God for granting us the means to provide meals for those who needed to be loved. I thanked God for all his provisions throughout our debt-free journey that had allowed us to reach this point of giving more freely to others. And I thanked God for this beautiful reminder that my actions as a mother are placing an imprint on the heart of my toddler.

I have, in the past months, shared this story on a few accounts. I shared it with our Financial Peace University class praying that it might give them hope – hope of a future where they too are debt free and able to give generously!

And I share this story today with you. If you are a parent, grandparent, aunt, uncle, teacher, or any individual who has contact with children, I pray that this encourages you to continue to model the love of Christ. You may not see your efforts come full circle, but we are all a part of this next generation's walk with Christ. And the part that each of us plays is important! My actions today could be paving the way for someone, possibly myself or another follower, to lead my daughter to give her life to Christ.

So I encourage you all. LOVE. Love like Christ loved the church. Love those around you and model that love constantly for the children in your life.

Those words ring in my mind, "Momma, take food?" While on that specific day, we weren't headed to deliver a meal, I forever want my response to be, "Yes, sweetheart, let's take food. Let's love someone in need today."

Tip #49
An Act of Service

Again, I need to precursor this by reminding you that I may be a bit biased as one of my top love languages is Acts of Service. However, I know that I am not alone in desiring this particular language of love. In fact, I really think that a study needs to be done examining the love languages of mothers. Let me explain...

Acts of Service has not always been my top love language. In fact, in college I much more deeply desired to be spoken the language of Physical Touch. However, when I became a mother and took on my callings as a mom and a wife, the amount of tasks I faced daily greatly increased. Slowly, my love languages began to reorder. Today, both my husband and I will attest that one of the greatest things someone could do for me to show me their love is to wash my dishes or fold my laundry – an act of service means so much to me.

In speaking with a number of my mom friends, I know that many of these other moms have experienced a similar transition. With the beginning of motherhood, comes the beginning of a new era of love languages – an era where Acts of Service is the number one love language for so many of these women.

So, I challenge you...look around. Find a mother, a friend, or a co-worker that you want to bless. Go to the individual's house and wash dishes, vacuum, clean bathrooms, dust, fold laundry, whatever that individual needs most! Bless them with an act, or acts, of service.

Maybe one of your friends is in the middle of a painting project, and for one night you go to that friend's house and paint alongside him or her. Not only will you be blessing that friend with an act of service, you too will be blessed from having the opportunity to give and the moments to fellowship together as you paint.

There are so many ways to give to another person through acts of service, whether it is inside housework or outside yard work. Maybe you even have a special talent such as plumbing or electrical capabilities, or sewing or photography skills that you can use to bless another. Be creative and you will discover so many ways to bless those around you!

Tip #50
The Power of Prayer

Is there a young person in your church headed on a mission trip to a third world country? Is there a benefit for a family in your community who lost their home to a fire? Is your heart aching with a desire to help, but your budget showing your inability to contribute financially at this time? This was totally us…and still is sometimes!

When you experience this heartache, please know that sometimes the most humbling and powerful way that you can give is through prayer. There are times, even now as we are debt free, when we are aware of a need but we don't have money to provide or we don't have the knowledge to know what is most needed. In these circumstances, we are brought to our knees.

The Bible constantly emphasizes the importance of prayer. Romans 12:12 reminds us, "Be joyful in hope, patient in affliction, and faithful in prayer." And Psalm 17:6 says, "I call on you, my God, for you will answer me; turn your ear to me and hear my prayer." In every part of your walk with the Lord, whether relating to giving or not, never hesitate to fall to your knees and have a conversation with your Savior.

Although, we are beginning to have more opportunities to give, there are always causes and people that we just don't have the financial means to give to. It is important to commit much prayer and thought into your giving because you want to give where you feel God is leading you to do so.

But, back to being unable to contribute financially…we get it! So, what do you do? You *never* underestimate the power of prayer! I think it is sometimes hard to remember that prayer is a way that we can give. We so many times want tangible results for our giving. We want to be able to see the things we give – to see how they are going to fill a need.

I remember the last Christmas before we became debt free. My husband and I, ever since we started dating, have had a tradition of packing shoeboxes for Operation Christmas Child. When we were dating, we packed two – one for him and one for me. When, I got pregnant with our first daughter, we packed three – one for him, one for me, and one for baby; and we continued that for our daughter's first Christmas. Now that we had a family of four, I was looking forward to packing four shoe boxes. Unfortunately, aside from our tithe, there wasn't room in our budget to buy items for filling shoeboxes. This was really hard for me. Why? Well, one I love traditions, and two, I feel that Operation Christmas Child is an important mission.

We still went to our church and helped pack shoe boxes and fellowshipped with our church friends, but we didn't contribute our own boxes. What we did contribute…our time spent packing and our prayers. I believe that those prayers, while not tangible, made a difference in this mission.

Every mission, every person, and every need must have an army of prayer warriors behind them. God commands us to pray. So, I encourage you, when faced with a need, fall to your knees. Rally behind that need in prayer. God will hear your prayers and will work in profound ways through your prayers.

closing

Not the End, But Rather a New Beginning

On the morning of March 1, 2017, as we all sat piled on the couch and made our final student loan payment, we could not have been happier. We were done! I remember feeling so relieved and thinking, *Wow! We really did it! We're done!* We had reached our goal. We had paid off our debt. That morning, it truly felt as if we had reached the 'end' of our journey.

But, in no way was that our 'end.' It was not our end because our financial goals – our financial journey – are so much more than being debt free. These goals go beyond this debt-free milestone to a future with a great retirement package that allows us to give generously, school funding for our children, and lots of opportunities for travel and experiences where we make unforgettable memories with our family.

I know this is not the end, but rather a beginning. You see, God used those 26 months to teach us how to care for our blessings, to bring us closer together as we worked toward a unified goal, and to instill in us healthy financial habits. I know this is not the end because, some time before we finished paying off our debt, God began nudging my husband to pursue a new career path. We tried to ignore the nudging (which we did effectively for quite a few months), but soon enough God got through to us when my husband lost his office job and he had to return to full-time paramedic status.

I know this is not the end because right now we are preparing for my husband to attend law school. We are planning to cash flow a law degree (that's three years of graduate school), meanwhile keeping me at home to raise our children. Although the numbers don't completely add up, we are surrendering this journey to our Savior, trusting that He has prepared us for the years to come. He has given us our faith, our financial knowledge and practices, and our strong communicative relationship. He has already been at work preparing us for three more years of some of the tightest budgets we've faced yet.

We are never done. Our financial journey is one that lasts a lifetime. (Well, beyond a lifetime actually. We want to be able to leave a legacy for our children – a legacy that will continue to give to both our children and our grandchildren.) Whether you are paying off debt, saving for a big purchase, planning for retirement, or trying to graduate college without student loans, I pray that this book has provided you with hope and encouragement on your journey.

If you want to be connected with a community of like-minded people (what better way to be encouraged?) or are searching for more financial tips, I would encourage you to consider taking part in the following:

23 & Debt Free

Take a moment to like and follow our Facebook page, *23 & Debt Free,* or follow us on Instagram, @23anddebtfree. On these pages we share lots of tips and tricks for saving you money. We provide financial resources and host live videos where we discuss different topics including budgeting, the Debt Snowball, getting your partner on board with the budget, and so much more! In addition, you become a part of a group of people that are all working towards financial goals of their own and are excited to encourage one another on this journey.

When I first began the page, *23 & Debt Free*, I followed my heart. I truly believed God was calling me, in that moment, to begin sharing our story with a larger audience of people. On this page, and now on our Instagram page as well, we share our hardships to inspire hope, share our successes to inspire endurance for those tackling a debt-free journey, and share our goals to inspire others to prepare for retirement and impart this financial wisdom upon their children. We share so many tips (big and small) that have played a part in our financial journey – tips that allow us to continue to live with financial freedom today. I am so excited about how God has already used these social media pages, this community of people, and our story. I hope that you will join us too!

In addition to providing information and hope on our social media pages, we also offer a variety of services which can be easily booked on our website, www.23anddebtfree.com. Our services are as follows:

Financial Coaching

One-On-One Financial Coaching provides you (and your spouse, if married) with a plan that will help you to succeed in your current financial situation. From making a budget and cutting costs to having a living will and life insurance in place, we will provide you with the resources you need to achieve financial freedom.

Keynote Speaking

We offer a couple of interactive lectures including 'Budgeting Made Simple' and 'Preparing for College.' The opportunities we have had to speak to audiences of a variety of ages have inspired us to continue sharing our story and teaching others, young and old, about making sound financial decisions.

Financial Peace University

Dave Ramsey offers a course called Financial Peace University (or FPU). This course is offered in churches, businesses, and communities all over the United States. And if you don't have access to a course in your area, you can take it online instead!

FPU, which you have heard me reference a few times in this book, is the best class on "adulting" that you could ever take! Over a period of nine weeks, Dave Ramsey leads you through weekly lessons covering topics such as budgeting, buying/selling a home, planning for retirement, paying off debt, finding the right insurance coverage, being aware of marketing strategies, negotiating, and so much more! No matter where you are in your financial journey, I know that you will gain knowledge from this class. We have helped co-lead this class twice now and each time I take away new and helpful information.

While FPU is offered both in person (in communities where someone is hosting the class) and online, I would encourage you to participate in a local group if at all possible. One of the best parts of FPU is surrounding yourself with a small group of people who will hold you accountable and encourage you as you walk through your financial journey. Having this connection with a small group is so crucial to your success – a connection that is not available online.

Other Events by Ramsey Solutions

Dave Ramsey, along with his team of professionals at Ramsey Solutions, hosts a number of events every year across the United States. These events focus on different topics including: money and marriage, teaching your kids about money, entrepreneurship, living debt free, and so much more. Check out Dave Ramsey's website for a full listing of all events! While some events are in-person events and may require a plane ticket for you to attend (which may not be feasible), they also live stream many of their events for a much reduced price.

Connect Within Your Church/Community

I cannot urge you enough to connect. Connect with other people on similar financial journeys. Connect with Christians. Connect with your church family. Connect with those that will support you and encourage you throughout this journey.

One of the most amazing groups of people we were surrounded by during our debt-free journey was our church small group. This was a group of about four to six couples that met on a weekly basis. While each of the couples in this group was walking a different financial journey, these couples were still an essential part of our debt-free journey. You see, while the couples in our small group may not have been encountering the same financial obstacles that we were facing, they each faced obstacles of their own (including financial obstacles and just the obstacles of life in general).

We shared the highs and the lows, and we felt loved and supported by this group. We knew that if anything happened, they had our back. The night that we had a small electrical fire in our home, who brought us supper and watched our children so we could clean up? Our small group. When we found out we were expecting our second child and we were feeling a bit scared, who celebrated with us and prayed for us? Our small group.

Church small groups are where 'church' really happens. It is within these groups that you are able to minister to and uplift others, and in-turn be ministered by others. I encourage you, if you are not already connected with a small group, to take time to find a small group in your church. The relationships and the support you will discover in a small group will provide you with the community that our hearts desire – a community that loves like Christ loved the church.

My prayer for my family as we continue our financial journey is that we would constantly seek God's will, blessing His kingdom with the firstfruits of our earnings. For this is not our money, but rather money that He has given to us. I pray that He will continue to open doors that allow us to share our story – the story of a journey that has strengthened our relationship as a couple, instilled many positive financial practices in our life, and allowed us to live free from debt.

May you too be blessed on your financial journey, wherever you are in that journey of a lifetime. I pray that God provides you with the discernment to understand where He is calling you to be and, if you are still in your debt-free journey, that you may soon experience the peace that comes with living free from debt. Many blessings upon you and your family!

annika's testimony

Following God's path is never easy. In fact, the Bible actually tells us that we as Christians will be persecuted for following Christ. When we began our debt-free journey, we knew that we were on a path that God had asked us to take. We were confident that we were following His will and the directions outlined in His book.

In Proverbs 22:7, we read, "The borrower is slave to the lender." (That's an important verse in our house...so important that our three-year-old has it memorized.) The act of borrowing is described as being an act folly. We also read in Proverbs 21:5, "The plans of the diligent lead surely to plenty, but those of everyone who is hasty, surely to poverty." We felt God calling us to no longer be enslaved, to no longer engage in folly, and to be diligent in preparing for our future.

Although our choices aligned with what God was asking of us, the journey itself was not easy. There were many times where we were looked upon by others as being weird. What we were doing – the decisions we were making regarding our finances – was not typical in today's world. We weren't normal. Because of this, there were times where we felt very isolated. We felt this way not only because people sometimes lacked understanding, but also because we were choosing to not engage in social activities that cost money as we were pouring all of our extra income into our debt. By the end of our journey, we had each other and we had our Lord and Savior, but some days it felt like we didn't have a lot of other people.

Through it all, I am so thankful for all that this journey has taught me. Truthfully, this journey was exceptionally hard for me. You see, I had married into the majority of this debt. Most of it wasn't "mine." However, in saying yes to becoming Logan's wife, I had chosen to take on this debt. We had chosen to combine our finances, an essential part of every marriage, and change our pronouns from "his money" and "her money" to "our money." Thus, we needed to tackle this debt together. It was now "ours." Nevertheless, I struggled with the journey of paying off "his" debt.

There were times that I questioned why I needed to sacrifice for someone else's debt. Then, one day in the midst of one of my pity parties, I was reminded of what Jesus Christ sacrificed for us. And what God sacrificed for us. He gave his begotten Son. His *only* Son. And sacrificed him on the cross to die for *our* sins. Sins that were not his. When I was reminded of this, I found myself being so very humbled and thinking how petty my frustrations were over sacrificing for this debt.

I feel so blessed to have faced this journey, and to continue to face adventures, with such an amazing teammate. However, Logan and I know full well that we could not have done this without first placing our trust in God. Ecclesiastes 4:12 says, "Though one may be overpowered, two can defend themselves. A cord of three strands is not quickly broken." Our chord has indeed proven to be 'not quickly broken' but rather has held steadfast, working together to pursue God's plan even in the face of adversity. I thank God for all His goodness, His provisions, and the teachings He has provided us through His word – goodness, provisions, and teachings that continue to guide our life together.

I have enjoyed the time I have spent writing this book. I love the work I do through 23 & Debt Free, and getting to put our story into 'book form' has been an incredible process. I still can't quite believe that this is actually happening.

However, if you know me, you know that my priorities in life are God, family, and work – in that order. So, although I have loved the time spent writing the pages of this book, I love being a wife and a mom even more! I look forward to continue pursuing my calling as a Proverbs 31 wife and mom. I feel overwhelmed at times by the task I have been given, but I am so incredibly grateful that God has entrusted me with two (soon to be three) beautiful children to teach and to love. I look forward to continue showing them the love of God, modeling His word, sharing his teachings and all that we have learned, and speaking truth into them in every adventure that the future may bring.

Wherever you are in your journey, no matter how the big the sacrifices may seem, I want you to remember that there is so much freedom in following God's plan. I will never forget the day that we clicked that button to submit our final debt payment. I remember this overwhelming feeling of relief sweeping over me. We were done! We would no longer be enslaved to anyone. "The borrower is slave to the lender." It felt amazing. I'm pretty sure I smiled like an idiot for a week. That feeling of relief – that feeling of freedom – has only continued. Since becoming debt free we have had so much more freedom to bless those around us with the abundant provisions that God has given to us. Thank you, Lord, for this journey and thank you for your goodness each and every day.

notes

Our Story

1. "Dave Ramsey's 7 Baby Steps," https://www.daveramsey.com/baby-steps/?ectid=30.31.13181&gclid=CjwKCAjwwuvWBRBZEiwALXqjw1IVq_lMBqQypFX3OWfa_P_3vZXD8bHpF1rufvpuBwX_8FH-cGayfRoCoFUQAvD_BwE.

   Baby Step 1: $1,000 cash in a beginner emergency fund
   Baby Step 2: Use the debt snowball to pay off all your debt but the house
   Baby Step 3: A fully funded emergency fund of 3 to 6 months of expenses
   Baby Step 4: Invest 15% of your household income into retirement
   Baby Step 5: Start saving for college
   Baby Step 6: Pay off your home early
   Baby Step 7: Build wealth and give generously

Chapter 1 – A Written Plan is Necessary

1. Shellie Warren, "10 Most Common Reasons for Divorce," *Marriage.com*, April 18, 2018, https://www.marriage.com/advice/divorce/10-most-common-reasons-for-divorce/.

Chapter 2 – Children are Expensive!

1. Diane Harris, "The Cost of Raising a Baby," *Parenting*, http://www.parenting.com/article/the-cost-of-raising-a-baby.

2. To use the First Year Baby Costs Calculator, visit the following link: https://www.babycenter.com/baby-cost-calculator.

> Please keep in mind that this calculator simply provides an estimate. Doing your own research about each specific baby product you will need will result in a more accurate budget. For example, the First Year Baby Costs Calculator estimates $100 for an infant car seat. In reality, we spent about $200 on our infant car seat. You can plug in your own numbers to give a more accurate estimate.
>
> I still appreciate this calculator, however, because it helps you think through the different baby items you might need to purchase.

3. Katie Adams, "Budgeting for a New Baby," *Investopedia*, August 1, 2017, https://www.investopedia.com/articles/pf/08/budgeting-for-baby.asp.

4. "Growing Up in Cloth," https://www.cottonbabies.com/collections/growing-up-in-cloth.

5. Cotton Babies' Seconds Sale, https://www.cottonbabies.com/collections/seconds-sale.

6. Trent Hamm, "How Much Does Breastfeeding Really Save?" *The Simple Dollar*, December 10, 2013, https://www.thesimpledollar.com/how-much-money-does-breastfeeding-really-save/.

Chapter 3 – Food: The Budget Buster

1. Quentin Fottrell, "Food for thought: 40% of groceries are thrown out every year," *MarketWatch*, June 5, 2018, https://www.marketwatch.com/story/this-is-why-americans-throw-out-165-billion-in-food-every-year-2016-07-22.

Chapter 4 – All Things Insurance

1. "Dave's Most Popular Money-Saving Tip," https://www.daveramsey.com/blog/independent-insurance-agent-popular-money-saving-tip.

2. "Is Whole Life Insurance Right for You?" *Consumer Reports*, April 6, 2015, https://www.consumerreports.org/cro/news/2015/04/is-whole-life-insurance-right-for-you/index.htm.

Chapter 8 – Rapid Fire: Bonus Tips for Slashing Costs

1. "About Amazon Prime," https://www.amazon.com/gp/help/customer/display.html?nodeId=201910360.

2. "The Latte Factor," *David Bach*, https://davidbach.com/latte-factor/.

about the author

Since marrying her husband in 2014, Annika has enjoyed taking on the roles of wife and mom. Annika primarily spends her days as a stay-at-home mom, or domestic engineer as her husband calls her, caring for the couple's two little girls. She has been actively involved in their family's church, helping to coordinate Financial Peace University classes and leading a small group of junior high and high school aged girls. She also enjoys being involved as an alumnus at the University of Jamestown. In her free time, she can be found playing piano or getting creative in her craft room.

Annika began 23 & Debt Free in 2017 when she felt God nudging her to share their family's story of becoming debt free. What began as a simple Facebook page to share tips has expanded to a growing business that continues to reach more people each day. From social media live videos to serving as a keynote speaker, Annika feels passionate about sharing their story and teaching people, young and old, about achieving financial freedom.

www.ingramcontent.com/pod-product-compliance
Lightning Source LLC
Chambersburg PA
CBHW051308220526
45468CB00004B/1262